DYE PAINTING!

Ann Johnston

No. 101

Detail of MERRY-GO-ROUND quilt.
Ann Johnston, ©1990.

Dye-painted silk appliquéd over pieced background; hand and machine quilted, beaded.

Detail of
BARS VARIATION:
SELF-PORTRAIT,
Ann Johnston, ©1990.

Fabric was dye
painted then washed,
pieced, decorated
with glitter paint, and
hand quilted.

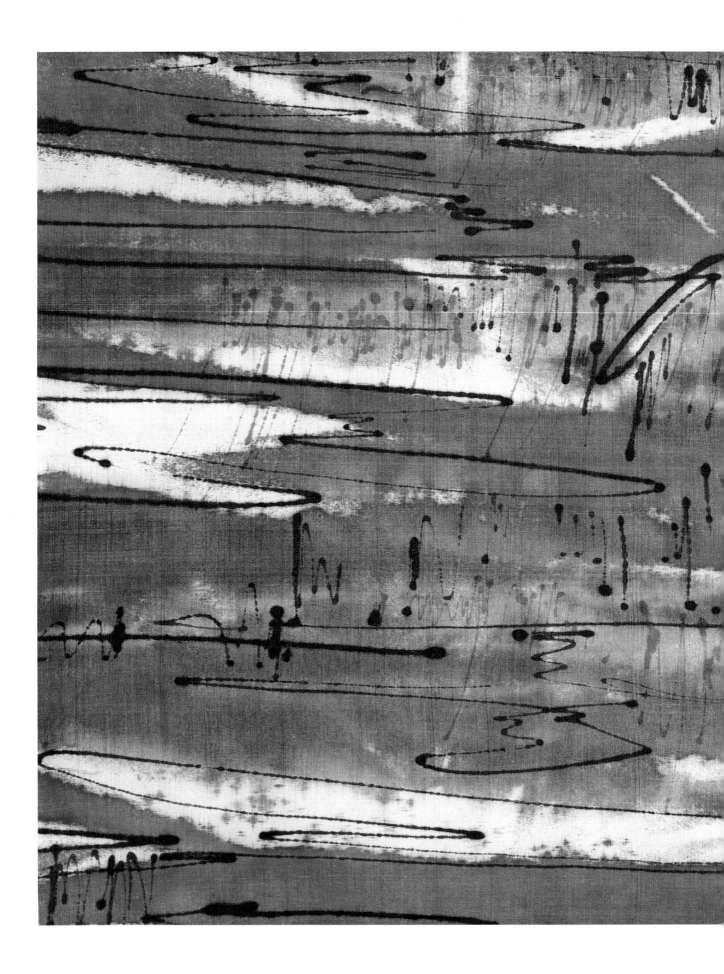

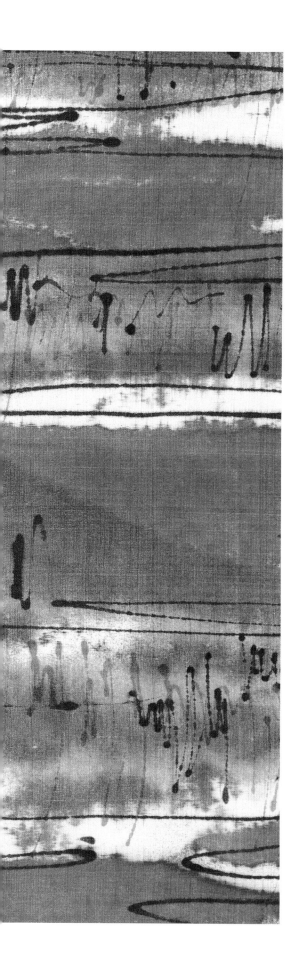

DYE PAINTING!

by

Ann Johnston

American Quilter's Society
P. O. Box 3290 • Paducah, KY 42002-3290

Library of Congress Cataloging-in-Publication Data

Johnston, Ann.
Dye Painting! / by Ann Johnston.

p.   cm.

Includes bibliographical references and index.
ISBN 0-89145-803-4: $19.95

1. Textile painting.   2. Dyes and dyeing – Textile fibers.
I. Title.
TT851.J64   1992
746.6 – dc20   92-23444
CIP

Additional copies of this book may be ordered from:

American Quilter's Society
P.O. Box 3290
Paducah, KY 42002-3290

@$19.95 Add $1.00 for postage & handling.

Previous page:
Tussah silk, folded and sprayed with dye; lines applied on the surface with a syringe.

Opposite page:
Silk broadcloth, bound on a wide tube with plastic string and painted with a medium/thin dye mixture.

DEDICATION

| To Jim

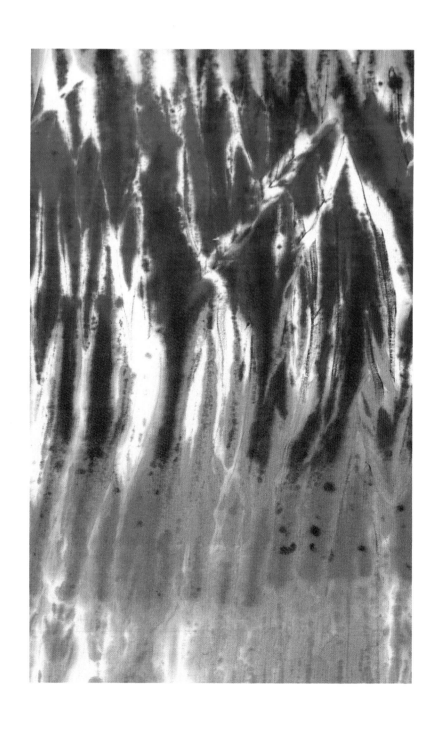

A special thanks to

Scott and Tod,

who dye paint with inspirational freedom.

Above:
MYSELF, MYSELF,
quilt, 20" x 23",
Tod Johnston (age 7),
1986. Dye painted and
hand quilted by Tod.

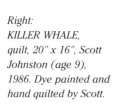

Right:
KILLER WHALE,
quilt, 20" x 16", Scott
Johnston (age 9),
1986. Dye painted and
hand quilted by Scott.

ACKNOWLEDGMENTS

I want to thank all of these people. They all helped my idea become a book in different ways, but their encouragement was the biggest help:

Bill Bachhuber, for taking all of the photographs except the clothing.
Don and Adelle Wiener, for advice on dye chemistry.
Dorothy Campbell and Diane Roberts, for their hand quilting.
Elaine Anne Spence, for the design and construction of garments.
Ann Marra, for her assistance with book design.
Pearl Kosta, for her assistance in the library.
Theresa Walla, for reading the manuscript.
Melanie Brown, for the use of her home.
Chet and Linda Skibinski, for help with the manuscript.
David Browne, for photographing the clothing.
Amile Cain and Pamela Montgomery, for modeling the clothing.
Duncan Slade and Gayle Fraas, for their workshop in 1984.

Contents

A STARTING PLACE

I am a dyer because I am a quiltmaker. The dye method I describe here has not only allowed me to have power over color, texture, and pattern in my quilts, but the process of dye painting itself is also a source of inspiration. The particular method I describe can be used to dye fabric for clothing and home decoration as well as for quilts and other types of fiber art. I consider the information in this book a starting place for the exploration of color and pattern on fabric without the expensive equipment, dangerous chemicals or specialized studio space required by many textile dyes. The dyer is not subject to the season of the year, the region of the country or the current fashions for choices in fabric color or design. Beginning dyers as well as others who already use the same dyes for immersion dyeing or batik will find this dye painting method a very useful tool. This book explains a simple recipe that allows many ways to apply the dye. Dye painting is a process that can be combined with other surface design techniques to create unique and specialized fabrics.

One of my primary goals has been to create washable fabric without changing its hand, that is, the fabric's surface texture and drape, for use in my quilts, garments, and other fabric projects. I started with a small bedroom studio and short, irregular amounts of time to work. Now I have a room with a sink in it, but the space is still lim-

Page 10:
Cotton, dye painted with sponge brushes and syringe, then sprayed with turquoise and fuchsia.

ited. My children are older, and I work on my quilts full time, but I still need to be able to do fine detail work over days and weeks, working on more than one project at a time if I wish. This particular method of direct application of dyes allows me to get to work at a moment's notice; the fabric, dyes, and other chemicals can be prepared ahead so they are ready to use. With this process, I also avoid having to use the steaming equipment that is required to fix some dyes.

It is important to me to be able to work without worrying about exposure to toxic or harmful substances. Many household cleaning agents and garden supplies are caustic, toxic, or both and are much more fearsome than fiber-reactive dyes. Procion® MX dyes and the auxiliaries required for the process presented in this book are considered low-hazard chemicals that simply require careful handling and common sense. Since the dye powder is very finely ground, it floats and could be inhaled. Contact with the powdered dye and chemicals can be prevented by the use of an appropriate dust mask. Use of the dyes in powder form is easily kept to a minimum because a dye stock can be mixed ahead and stored in the refrigerator.

I would like to emphasize at the beginning that this method is not the only way to apply fiber-reactive dyes. There are many different kinds of reactive dyes, each requiring different conditions for maximum reaction of the dye and fiber. For each reactive dye class there are several different methods to fix the color. Don't panic if you read conflicting information or different recipes. These dyes have only been made available to studio artists gradually over the last 20 years, and the distributors' directions are often limited to their own needs, uses, and experience. The recipe presented in this book is a chemically correct way to create colorfast fabric. I did not invent it, but I have adapted it to be as convenient as possible. In exploring its applications, I have learned about its potential and found some of its limits. In addition to the basic information necessary for the dye painting process, this book addresses the technical points that dyers should know in order to adapt the process to their own artistic needs. Many of the things I have learned from experience are presented in this book, to save the reader the time it took me to discover them.

In addition to being a practical guide to exploring color and design directly on fabric, this book is a detailed resource you can use as more technical questions arise. The colors in the photographs demonstrate the effectiveness of the dye recipe – all the fabrics have been thoroughly washed unless noted in the caption – but I do want the reader to realize that there are too many variables for me to guarantee results that might be expected. As with everything else, experience makes the process easier, the tools more accurate, and the results more predictable. The exercises in the chapters about colors and applications are designed to encourage you to play with the dyes and learn from direct experience before starting a special project. Dye painting offers you an opportunity to create original fabric which you can use for greater self-expression in your work.

Below:
I sometimes use the computer to create my fabric designs and plan the colors I will dye for my quilts. See INSIDE THE HEXAGON, page 63.

Chapter 1

WHAT IS DYE PAINTING?

About The Process
About The Dyes

ABOUT THE PROCESS

There are basically two ways to dye fabric: you can submerge it in a dye solution or you can paint the dye directly on the fabric. With the first method, called immersion dyeing, the fabric is submerged in a solution of dye, water, and other chemicals such as salt and soda ash, which fix the dyes. When using this method, a large amount of water in relation to dye is used, and time must be allowed for the dye to react with the fabric.

Dye painting refers to all of the other ways that dye can be applied to fabric. Dye can be painted on with a brush, sprayed, stamped, stenciled, silkscreened, or applied through any combination of these techniques. In dye painting, a much smaller amount of water in relation to dye is used, and the necessary chemicals can be mixed in with the dye or put on the fabric. As with immersion dyeing, time must be allowed for the reaction to occur.

The most significant advantage of applying the dye directly by dye painting is the fact that with this process the dyer can control exactly how and where the dye is put, and can immediately see the approximate hue, value, and placement of the dye. Dye painting also allows many options, such as very fine lines on heavy fabric, smooth color gradations and shading, and designs without outlines. To achieve the desired effects, the dye solution can be mixed very thick, like pudding, or thin, like water, and can be applied to wet or to dry fabrics. The final effect can be bold and blurry or precise with hard edges. One design can even be applied over another, taking advantage of the transparency of the colors.

Traditionally, melted wax or other thick liquid resists were used to control the flow of dye on the surface of a fabric to create a pattern. These substances that protect areas of a fabric from dye were used to outline designs or block out areas. With dye painting it is not necessary to use resists because the dye can be mixed to a consistency that allows you to control its flow. However, resists can be used in conjuction with this method of direct application, to achieve special effects.

ABOUT THE DYES

This direct method uses fiber-reactive dyes which are synthetic dyes that can be used with natural fibers – cotton, viscose rayon, wool, silk. Fiber-reactive dyes produce bright, even colors in a full range and mix well. They are safe, economical, easy to use, and resist fading. The molecules of fiber-reactive dyes chemically react with fiber molecules, uniting through electron sharing, the strongest type of chemical bond. Since this bond is not water-soluble, these dyes are colorfast, and because fiber-reactive dyes unite with the fiber molecules rather than

Opposite page: Cotton broadcloth, folded and sprayed with turquoise, fuchsia, and yellow, and then embellished with black dye applied with a squeeze bottle.

simply lying on the surface, when the process is complete, the surface texture of the dyed fabric is the same as before dyeing. The only disadvantage of these dyes is that several washings are needed to completely remove all unfixed dye, so the color will not migrate during later washing.

The most often used fiber-reactive dyes are Procion® MX, Cibacron® F, Liquid Reactive, and Procion® H. Each requires different conditions for maximum reaction between dye and fibers, so it is important to know which type you are using. That is not always easy. Procion® MX dyes, for example, are made by only one manu-

facturer in the United States and are sold in huge quantities to commercial dyers. The studio artist is only able to buy this dye from distributors who have repackaged it in smaller quantities and added their own labels. The distributors' packages may not even have the word Procion® on them, and the descriptions of the dye and its use may vary, depending on the experiences of the distributors. Because each dye has a different rate of reactivity (time required for reaction), the dyer should buy from companies indicating exactly which dye is in the package.

Right:
Detail from GLYPH I,
Ann Johnston, ©1987.

Dye has been
smoothed on cotton
sateen with a brush,
to create shaded
areas.

Procion® MX is the type of dye I use for dye painting because it is the most versatile, functional and economical dye available. It is the most highly reactive of the four types of dye, which means that it reacts the most quickly and with the least amount of heat. It can be cured without special heat or steam treatment in less than 24 hours. Cibacron® F requires about twice as long to cure at room temperature; however, it is still considered a very reactive dye. Liquid Reactive dyes are only moderately reactive, and Procion® H dyes have a very low reactivity rate, $\frac{1}{50}$th the rate of Procion® MX. These last two dyes require the use of heat or a very strong alkali to fix the color.

The reactivity rate of a dye also affects the length of time the dye powder can be stored mixed with water. The higher the reactivity rate, the more quickly the dye molecules will bond with water molecules and no longer be available to react with fiber molecules. Many recipes for Procion® MX dye call for measuring the dye powder and water with the auxiliary chemicals each time the dyer wants to work, but it is more convenient to have them pre-mixed. It is possible to keep a concentrated dye stock solution (minus fixative) in the refrigerator, because the shelf life of the dye/water stock is dependent on its reactivity rate and temperature.

Procion® MX dyes are room temperature dyes; that is, the dye molecules move around and react at temperatures between 70°F and 105°F. This means that if you mix the dye with very hot tap water, over 110°F, you may destroy the reactivity of the dye. Likewise, if the dyed fabric is left in a cold room to cure, below 65° for example, the reaction will virtually stop. If the dye-and-water solution is refrigerated, the practical storage time will be lengthened because the reactivity of the dye is slowed by cool temperatures. At room temperature, the dye will gradually react with the water and although it will still appear to be a deep color, the dye molecules will no longer be able to bond with the fibers and they will wash out. I find I can keep the refrigerated dye stock a month with only slight color loss and often use

it for up to five months with satisfactory results. Because studio practices vary, I recommend that the dyer keep fabric samples over time to determine the differences between freshly mixed dye stock and older stocks.

The dye process may sound complicated, but it is really like a good food recipe – the more often you use it, the easier it will be to follow. With dye painting, you open a whole array of color and design possibilities for fabric projects. The fabrics you create will be as colorfast as those you buy in the store – or more so – and they will have the same drape, weight, and texture as the original fabrics.

Below:
Detail of ORCHID IV,
Ann Johnston, ©1991.
Hand quilted by
Dorothy Campbell.

Dye has been painted on silk broadcloth in a hard-edge design. Note the absence of the outlines created by resist dye techniques.

Chapter 2

The METHOD

Overview

Steps In The Process

Silk, A Simpler Method

Summary Of Recipes

OVERVIEW

Dye painting involves using Procion® MX dyes, water, urea, thickener, fabric pre-treated with soda ash, and a cure of 4 to 24 hours at room temperature. No resist is required to control the flow of the dye; no steaming is required to fix the colors.

The first three steps, which all involve measuring, can be done well ahead of time: the fabric is soaked in a soda ash/water solution and dried, the print mix is dissolved and allowed to thicken, and the dye/water stock is mixed and refrigerated. When it is time to paint, the dyer mixes the dye stock with the print mix to create the desired color and value and then applies it to the fabric. Next, the dyed fabric is left at room temperature to allow the chemical reaction between the dye and fibers to occur. To complete the process, the fabric is washed thoroughly to remove all soda ash, thickener, and unfixed dye.

STEPS IN THE PROCESS

For the best results, use fabric that has no sizing or permanent press treatment. If the fabric has been treated or you are uncertain, scour the fabric in hot water, soda ash (also referred to as washing soda or as sodium carbonate) and Synthrapol® SP (a detergent formulated for use with Procion® dyes). Use ½ teaspoon of each for every pound of fabric (1-3 yards) in the washing machine. The combination of soda ash and Synthrapol® SP is especially effective in removing surface treatments on fabric.

Even when I buy fabric that has been prepared for dyeing, I shrink it first, because the fabric will be washed in hot water after it is dyed and it will shrink unevenly in length and width. I failed to pre-shrink fabric the year I made fabric boxes for everyone at Christmas. I drew the pattern on the fabric and dyed the designs to fit. Needless to say, when I washed out the excess dye in hot water, the fabric shrunk, so it no longer fit the cardboard pieces. Because the fabric didn't shrink symmetrically, reducing the pattern didn't solve the problem. Remember that even one wash and dry doesn't always completely shrink fabric.

• STEP 1: PREPARE THE FABRIC.

Soda ash is an alkali that is needed to trigger the dye-fiber reaction and make the bond permanent. In this no-steam dyeing method, it is applied to the fabric rather than mixed with the dye. Start with dry fabric. Activate it by soaking thoroughly in a solution of 9 tablespoons soda ash per gallon of water. The treated fabric can be dyed wet, damp, or dry. Excess soda solution can be spun out in a washing machine because it is the same alkali often present in laundry detergent. Be sure your washing machine does not spray in clean water during the spin cycle! I

Opposite page:
Cotton broadcloth stamped and painted then sprayed with dye.

do not put soda-soaked fabric in the dryer because soda would stay in the dryer and never be rinsed away. If it were picked up by clothes, it would become an irritant; it would be as if the clothes had been washed and dried without rinsing out the detergent.

Once dry, the fabric can be ironed smooth, but only at a medium setting, because the washing soda will turn dark at a high temperature. However, I find that a light scorch mark will often wash out with the excess dye. The alkali solution can be used indefinitely, and added to as its volume lessens. I usually keep a covered gallon jar of the solution, mixed and ready. The dry, treated cotton and rayon can also be kept indefinitely, ready to dye. If you wish to work on wet fabric, dyeing can begin once the fabric has been soaked in soda.

There are other methods in which the soda ash is mixed directly with the dye. The dye in these mixtures has a very short shelf life and the fabric may require heat or steam to fix the colors. See Appendix A for more information on variations on this method.

• STEP 2: MAKE THE PRINT MIX.

When the fabric is soaked as described above, the correct amount of alkali is put on the fibers for the dye reaction to occur. The print mix is the medium that contains urea in the correct proportions needed for the dye process. Urea is a common ingredient in hand lotions and fertilizers; it is a nitrogen compound used as a humectant to attract and keep in moisture. Sodium alginate (also called keltex) is the thickener for the print mix. It is an antimigrant extracted from seaweed which allows the artist to control the flow of the dye when it is on the fabric. The amount of sodium alginate can be adjusted down to none, according to the desired effect. Two other ingredients are often used in the print mix. Sodium hexametaphosphate or "metaphos" is used to smooth the flow of the sodium alginate. It is often referred to as Calgon®, a water softener. Ludigol® (also called Resist Salt L) is a mild oxidizing agent that is used to improve the curing of the dyes. It is a

dyeing assistant, essential to direct application of Procion® H dyes and possibly helpful in direct dyeing of brighter Procion® MX colors. I have seen various recipes that do not contain this ingredient, but I have always used it, and I like the results.

There are two ways to prepare the print mix: buy the ingredients dry and pre-mixed, and add water, or buy and measure the ingredients separately and mix with water. After 10 years of mixing all the ingredients from scratch, I find using the prepared mix the easiest. The dry mix is very finely ground and it seems to dissolve in less time. PRO Print Paste Mix SH, available from PRO Chemical and Dye, Inc., makes a very thick mix at 5½ tablespoons of dry mix to 1 cup water. To thin this mixture and keep the proportions correct for the dye process, use a solution of urea and water, 7 teaspoons of urea per cup of water. Other distributors have various ways of packaging the print mix, sometimes with the thickener in a separate package so that you can add the amount you wish. Just be sure you know what the ingredients are in the mix.

If you have the ingredients on the shelf and wish to mix from scratch, here is the recipe. Dissolve 1½ teaspoons of metaphos, 1½ teaspoons of Ludigol®, and 6½ tablespoons of urea in 3 cups of hot water, in that order. The water will cool quickly as the urea dissolves. Add 0-8 teaspoons of sodium alginate SH, while stirring constantly. Shake vigorously and add water to make 1 quart. Let it sit at least six hours or overnight; the lumps will eventually dissolve. This mix can also be thinned with urea water as described above.

Once prepared, the print mix and urea water can be mixed in any proportion with each other and with the dye stock. I usually work with the print mix in several consistencies, so I prepare some mix very thick and some less thick, and keep the urea water ready to use as needed.

• STEP 3: MAKE THE DYE STOCK.

The dye stock is made up of dye powder, water, and urea. The urea allows more dye to be dissolved in a small amount of water than would be possible without it. The dye stock is very concentrated, and a little goes a long way, so I only mix small quantities. I recommend starting with ¼ cup of each primary color, which would mean cutting this recipe in half. Mix ½ cup of water (85°-110°) with 2½ tablespoons of urea. Add 1 level tablespoon of dye powder. Cover and shake.

Remember:

1. When handling the dye powders, use gloves and an approved dust mask.

2. Refrigerate the stock when it is not in use.

• STEP 4: MIX DYE STOCK AND PRINT MIX.

Mix approximately equal parts dye stock and print mix to make a dark value of the color. I do this by eye, not measuring. Stir well. Lighter values of the colors are achieved by adding more print mix. Darker values can be achieved by adding less print mix or overdyeing an area after it is dry. I usually mix only the amount of dye I plan to use in a day; practice has enabled me to match the color to my satisfaction at a later time. If you wish to store the mixed color (dye stock plus print mix), try refrigeration and test your results. Keep a record book of washed and unwashed samples so you can determine the limits of storage (see photo, page 22). You may find, especially with light colors, that for you the difference between a one-day-old color and three-day-old color is not significant enough to matter.

• STEP 5: APPLY THE DYE TO THE FABRIC.

The dye stock/print mix combination can be applied to soda-soaked fabric in just about any way the desired effect can be created. Very fine lines, with a #000 brush, or bold lines, with a wide sponge roller, are both possible. The artist can use a stamp, silk screen, sponge, wood block, or squeeze bottle. The mixture can also be sprayed, but that must be done with good ventilation and a special mist/vapor mask so no mist is inhaled. The colors can be applied in layers, wet or dry, within reasonable limits. The fabric can be cured, washed, soaked and

dyed again. Some of the many options will be described and illustrated in Chapter 5.

• STEP 6: CURE THE FABRIC.

Three conditions are required to maximize the dye-fiber reaction: moisture, room temperature, and time. The molecules of dye cannot move and react without moisture. When there is no movement, there is little contact between the dye and fiber molecules, so little dye-fiber bonding occurs, and as a result very little coloring occurs. Actually, the level of moisture required is very small. *The fabric could feel dry to the touch and still have enough moisture for the reaction to occur.* If the fabric becomes completely dry, the reaction will stop, so the drying of the dyed fabric should be monitored. An arid climate, forced air heat, and air conditioning all influence the drying time of the fabric. I usually wait until it feels only slightly moist, then cover it lightly with plastic. This way large pieces can be stacked in layers and even rolled without worrying that the dye will bleed or drip or move. Of course, if you want the colors to bleed into each other and blend on the fabric, immediately covering the piece of fabric will encourage that to happen. If the fabric is very sparsely dyed without much liquid, I sometimes cover part of it while I work or cover it immediately after painting to be sure there is enough moisture retained in the fabric.

Room temperature, 70°-105°, is another condition for the dye-fiber reaction; if it is too cold, the reaction is slowed or stopped. If you paint all day and your studio gets very cold at night, less dye will fix with the fibers than if the fabric remained at normal room temperature for the whole curing time. I have had good results with a wide range of temperatures. When I have a piece curing with very intense colors, I pay attention to the temperature, and in the winter I keep the space heater on in my studio for at least eight hours after I've applied the last dye.

The third condition necessary for maximum dye reaction is time. The dye and fiber molecules need time to mix and react. The minimum time is about four hours, but the reaction can continue to occur for up to 24 hours. I usually wait at least overnight, but sometimes it is several days before I get to the wash-out process. Sometimes I paint, let a piece cure overnight (slightly moist and at room temperature), and then let it dry, hanging it on my studio wall for days or months before I am ready to paint more dye on it. If the print mix has been used in thick layers, it may dry in a whitish crust. Thick layers of print mix can keep later layers of dye from penetrating, so you may want to wash the fabric and soak it again before applying more dye. Each time I paint, I make sure that the fabric cures in conditions within the necessary range. Actually, though, I enjoy the process without worrying too much about the conditions, because the only effect of variations in time, temperature, and moisture is that slightly more or less dye washes out.

• STEP 7: WASH OUT EXCESS DYE.

The alkali and any unfixed dye must be thoroughly removed from the fabric, or it will continue to bleed out in later washings. Even though some dye molecules do not react with the fiber, they have an affinity for it, so vigorous washing is necessary to remove them, using heat, agitation and detergent. Start with room-temperature water to dissolve the alkali, 70°-105°. When the water is fairly clear, wash the fabric in gradually warmer water and Synthrapol® SP, which is formulated for use with reactive dyes. Work up to hot water, washing by hand. When I am sure the alkali and much of the dye are out, I often use the washing machine for the last few washes.

The deeper the colors, the more care and the more washes you will need to give the fabric. Several short washes are better than one long wash to remove the unreacted dye that has gone into the water. If the fabric is not agitated or stays tangled in hot water, the dye can transfer wherever the fabric touches. If this happens, a hot wash in Synthrapol® SP can remove the transferred dye, unless a lot of alkali was present when the dye transferred. Synthrapol® SP is a surfactant that keeps particles in suspension and off the fibers. It has also helped me remove excess dye from commercially produced fabrics that have bled.

Iron the damp fabric between two clean pieces of cotton to see whether all the unfixed dye is washed out. Of course, the fabric can then be dried and soaked in soda and dyed again.

Keep samples. Occasionally tear a 2" strip from the edge of the dyed fabric before washing, and later attach it to the washed piece for a visual reminder of unwashed colors and values.

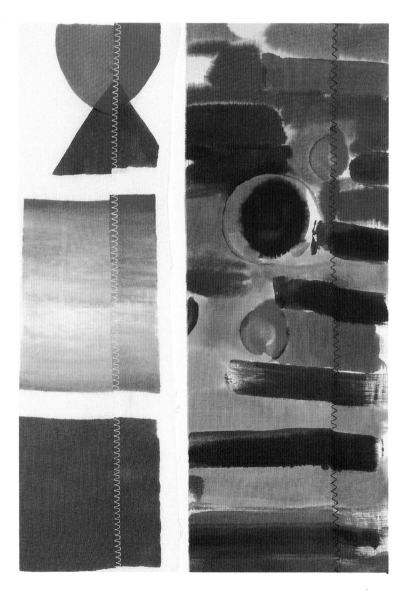

Doing this will train your eye to anticipate the slightly lighter values of the washed fabric. It will also be a check-up on the freshness of your dye stock and the correctness of your curing process. If there is more than a slight difference in the values, review all of the above steps to determine what you did differently.

SILK, A SIMPLER METHOD

The method described above will dye cotton, viscose rayon, and linen because they are cellulose fibers. It also dyes silk, even though silk is a protein fiber that normally requires acid as the dye assistant. Silk is a special protein fiber because it is a secretion, not a hair growth, so the silk fiber molecules have the same reactive groups as the cellulose fibers of cotton and rayon. When dye painting silk, however, acid can be used as the dye assistant instead of alkali. This allows the dyer to skip the soak in soda ash and mix the acid directly into the print mix. When the alkali method is used with silk, be aware that alkali can damage silk fibers if the piece is stored for long periods of time and if any dampness is present. Following is a shorter process for silk, following the same step-by-step method as for cotton.

• STEP 1: PREPARE THE FABRIC.

Silk often contains a lot of sizing and will shrink, so it should be scoured in hot water, Synthrapol® SP and soda ash. Silk is degummed in 185° water to prepare it for spinning, so do not worry about using hot water. However, silk is sensitive to sudden drops in temperature, so avoid putting silk directly from hot to cold water. Reduce the temperature of the water gradually.

• STEP 2: MAKE THE PRINT MIX.

Prepare the print mix according to Step 2 described on page 20. Then add 2 teaspoons of 56% acetic acid per quart of print mix. This concentration of acetic acid is about 11 times the strength of cooking vinegar. If urea water is used to thin the print mix, add acetic acid in the same proportions to it also (2 teaspoons of 56% acetic acid per quart). Citric acid crystals may be substituted for the acetic acid, 4 teaspoons per quart. Both acids are available from dye distributors.

Sodium alginate SH is a high-viscosity, low-solids thickener for cotton, rayon, and silk. This means that it doesn't take very much powder to make a very thick mixture; each particle swells to many times its size. I use it for all my fabric and it works well.

If very fine-line definition is needed, sodium alginate SH can be replaced by sodium alginate F, which is a low-viscosity, high-solids thickener often used for silk. Sodium alginate F might be needed when a very detailed silk screen image is printed, because each particle swells less. High-solids means it takes more particles to make the same thickness. Making the print mix from scratch would require more than twice the amount of sodium alginate F to achieve the same thickness as with sodium alginate SH. The amount of metaphos in the recipe is determined by the amount of thickener, so it should be doubled to 3 teaspoons per quart of water. When dye painting on a very delicate silk, sodium alginate F may wash out easier than sodium alginate SH.

• STEP 3: MAKE THE DYE STOCK.

Follow the same process described in Step 3 on page 20.

• STEP 4: MIX THE DYE STOCK AND PRINT MIX.

Follow the same process described in Step 4 on page 21.

Optional: To help the dye penetrate into the fibers, add 1 teaspoon Synthrapol® SP (or less) per quart of print mix. The Synthrapol® SP slightly counteracts the thickener and increases the flow of dye in the fibers, so experiment.

• STEP 5: APPLY THE DYE TO FABRIC.

The same applications are possible. Remember that any time urea water is used, it should have the acid in it also, in the same proportions – 2 teaspoons of 56% acetic acid or 4 teaspoons of citric acid crystals per quart.

• STEP 6: CURE THE FABRIC.

The acetic acid mixture is not as strong as the alkali mixture, so more time is required to fix the colors. Allow 24 hours at room temperature and slightly moist conditions. The longer time interval requires more attention to keeping the fabric from becoming completely dry. Sometimes I steam iron the dyed silk or put it in the dryer if I am working for a very deep black.

• STEP 7: WASH OUT EXCESS DYE.

Follow the same process as for cotton, as described in Step 7, page 22; just be careful to change the temperature of the water gradually, because sudden changes in temperature can damage the silk fibers. Keep samples.

Right:
Detail of monoprinted
silk broadcloth.

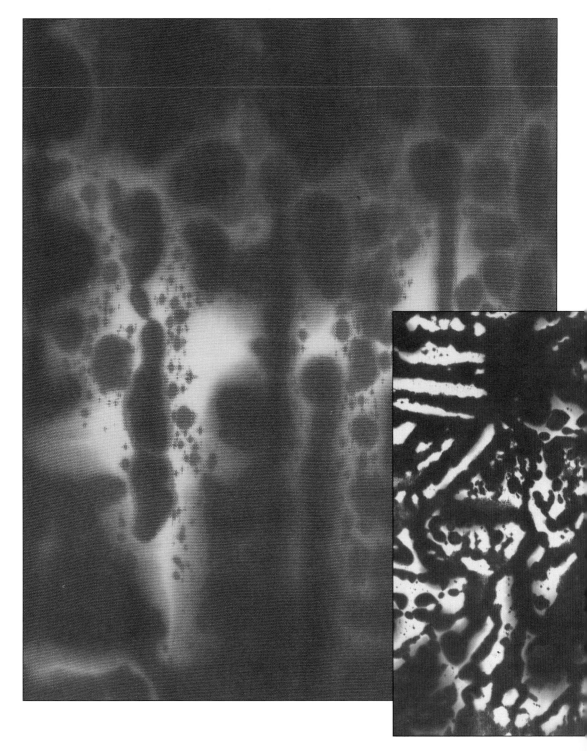

Summary Of Recipes
For Dye Painting Cotton, Silk & Rayon

- STEP 1: PREPARE THE DRY FABRIC.
  Fabric scouring solution
    (necessary only if fabrics have a finish),
  To scour 1 pound fabric (3-4 yards cotton):
    ½ teaspoon soda ash
    ½ teaspoon Synthrapol® SP
    Hot water (over 135°)
  Alkali solution for pre-treating fabric:
    9 tablespoons soda ash
    1 gallon water

- STEP 2: MAKE THE PRINT MIX.
  Print mix, shortcut:
    5½ tablespoons PRO Print Paste Mix SH
    1 cup warm water
  Urea water to thin print mix:
    7 teaspoons urea
    1 cup hot water

Print mix from scratch:
    3 cups hot water
    1½ teaspoons metaphos
    1½ teaspoons Ludigol®
    6½ tablespoons urea
    0-8 teaspoons sodium alginate SH
    Additional water to make 1 quart total

- STEP 3: MAKE THE DYE STOCK.
    ½ cup water, 85°-110°
    2½ tablespoons urea
    1 tablespoon Procion® MX dye powder

- STEP 4: MIX TOGETHER DYE STOCK & PRINT MIX.
    Equal parts of each for dark values
    Use more print mix for lighter values

- STEP 5: APPLY THE DYE MIXTURE TO THE
  TREATED FABRIC.
    See Chapter 5.

- STEP 6: CURE.
    Room temperature, 70°-105°
    4 to 24 hours
    Slight moisture in fabric

- STEP 7: WASH OUT.
    Thorough rinse in lukewarm water
    Final wash in hot water, 140° or higher
    1 teaspoon per gallon Synthrapol® SP *or*
      1-2 tablespoons per machine load
    Continuous agitation
    Warm rinse

(Post a copy where you work, for reference.)

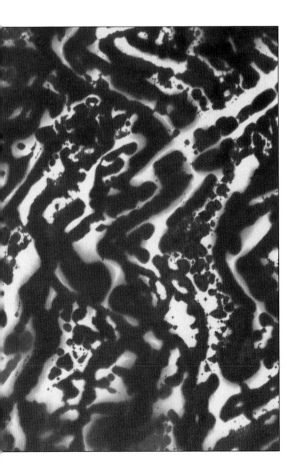

Left:
Silk broadcloth monoprinted from a dye pattern created on a smooth work surface.

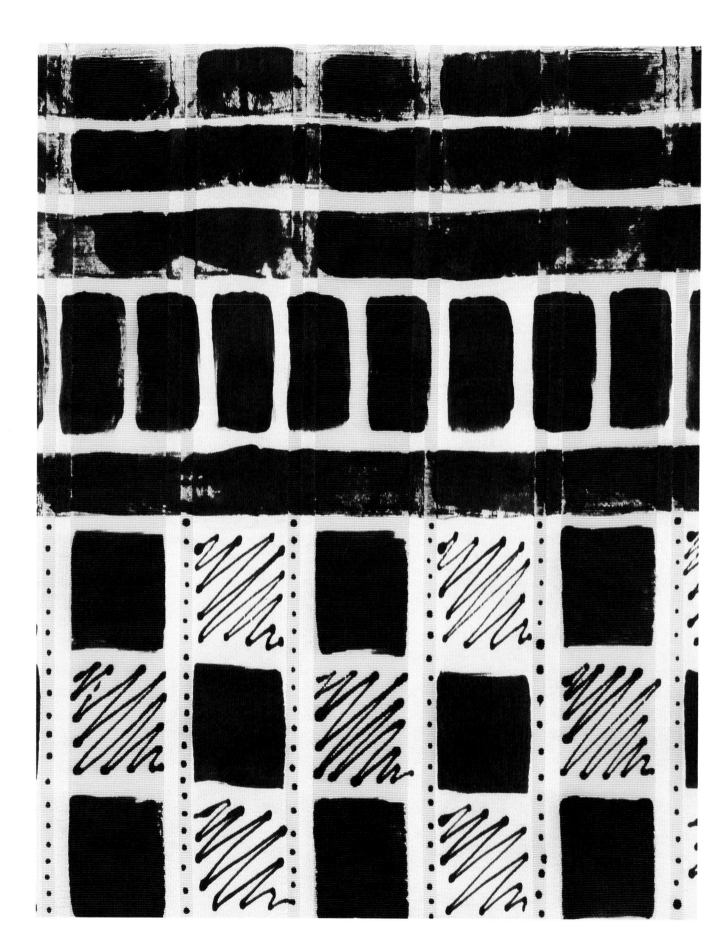

Chapter 3

THE MATERIALS

Safety	Fabric
Basic Supplies List	Tools
Availability Of Supplies	Work Space

SAFETY

Procion® MX dyes and the chemicals used with them are considered safe for their proper use. Any chemical can be misused and become toxic – even something as ordinary as salt, for example. Like all the other chemicals we use in our daily lives, dyes and their auxiliaries should be handled with care.

1. Do not allow chemicals to get into the eyes. If they do, wash your eyes thoroughly with clean water and call for medical advice. Consider wearing safety goggles while measuring dye and alkali powders if you wear contact lenses.

2. The dye and alkali powders are very light so their dust floats up easily. To reduce exposure, use a disposable fiber dust mask approved for use with dyes. Handle the dry powders carefully, avoiding excessive stirring and keeping the lids on the jars as much as possible. Occasional cases of allergic reaction to these dyes and chemicals have been reported among people who have had prolonged contact in industrial situations.

3. Although it has been found that these powders are unlikely to be absorbed by the human skin, prolonged or repeated contact with the skin should be avoided. Use gloves, especially when measuring and washing.

4. All containers and measuring tools used in dye painting should be reserved for use only with the chemicals. Clearly label all containers. Separate work spaces should be used for food preparation and art work, to prevent contamination of either.

5. Keep the dry chemicals well out of the reach of children. Have fabric, dye stocks, and print mix fully prepared before dye painting with children.

6. These dyes are not considered hazardous waste, and such small quantities of dye and alkali are used with the direct application method that disposal of the chemicals involved is not a problem.

I dye much of my fabric in the same workroom where I do my designing and sewing, so I am doubly motivated to keep all of the chemicals under control. It doesn't take much work to manage them neatly, without spills and airborne powder.

One of the best ways to minimize spreading dye powder is to buy it in wide-mouth, screw-top containers instead of plastic bags. When you are using jars, the dye can be measured and the lid replaced quickly, with none of the static of plastic bags, and the outside of the container can easily be kept clean. My paying attention to the subject of safety with the chemicals used in dye painting has made me more careful with the other chemicals I use around the house, many of which have dusts, fumes, and mists that can be harmful and should be avoided.

Opposite page:
Heavy rayon with a woven design, dye painted with brush and syringe.

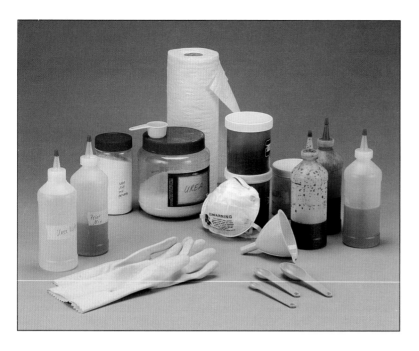

Above:
Powdered dye in
wide-mouth jars,
dust mask, and other
supplies.

Right:
These two pieces of
cotton broadcloth
were dyed with
the same dye, and
cured in the same
conditions. The fabric
on the right shows
darker colors because
it is mercerized.

BASIC SUPPLIES LIST

Procion® MX dyes, 2 oz. each:
red, yellow, blue
PRO Print Paste Mix SH, 8 oz
Urea, 1 pound
Soda ash, 1 pound
Synthrapol® SP, 1 pint
Gloves
Dust mask
Plastic measuring spoons and cups
Plastic squeeze bottles
Recycled containers with lids
Funnel
Plastic palettes, plates, or cups
Fabric
White work surface
Plastic wash basin
Gallon jar
Brushes
Masking tape
Paper towels
Notebook to store samples

AVAILABILITY OF SUPPLIES

Procion® MX dyes, auxiliary chemicals, and other supplies are available through many dye distributors' catalogues, some of which are

listed in Appendix B. Large art supply stores also carry them. All of the supplies listed can be purchased at a reasonable cost. To begin, look for a starter kit containing small quantities of the three primary colors, alkali, urea, print mix, and Synthrapol® SP. I buy dust masks from a dye distributor in order to get ones with the appropriate safety designation. Distributors also sell many other supplies you might find convenient. Masonite with one side enameled white is an easy-to-clean white work surface, and is sold at lumber yards under various brand names. The biggest variable in expense is fabric, which you can buy anywhere. I find that I can get the best prices mail-ordering in quantity.

FABRIC

The kind of fabric you buy to paint will depend on your plans for it. The following are some things to consider.

1. Many fine cottons cannot be hand quilted, so I always get a sample first and feel it with a needle as well as with my fingers.

2. Mercerized cotton has been treated with

a caustic alkali in a process that increases the fabric's strength, luster, and affinity for dyes. It rounds out the fibers and, with the same amount of dye, the fabric looks about 25% darker than unmercerized cotton.

3. If you work on bleached cotton, the colors will look different than if you work on unbleached or greige (unfinished) cotton.

4. Thick fabric will absorb more dye than thin fabric and will feel different to paint.

5. A fabric with a tight weave will often seem to have darker colors than a fabric with a thinner weave because there are more fibers per square inch to react with the dye.

6. A cotton blend can be dyed with this dye process; however, the dye will react only with the cotton fibers and not with the polyester, nylon, or other synthetic fibers. Try a sample. The colors will be lighter, in proportion to the amount of synthetic fiber in the blend.

7. Commercial prints can be dye painted. Remember that the colors are transparent and that results will depend on the colors already on the fabric.

8. Silk, viscose rayon (made from wood fibers), and linen can be dyed using the same basic dye method described in Chapter 2.

9. Consider buying ready-made clothing and dye painting it. Remember that the thread will not be dyed if it is synthetic.

Above:
Some of the tools you might use to apply the dyes.

TOOLS

The dyes can be applied with just about any tool. Some of the ones I've used are listed below. The main thing to think about is what effect you want to create. Sea sponges and synthetic sponges have different textures and costs, so use the one that suits your purpose and budget. You might need to use a stiffer bristle brush when working with very thick print mix than when painting delicate lines with a thinner mixture. I have had good results from all kinds of brushes, but I would avoid buying the very expensive natural fiber brushes such as sable, because the alkali in the dye painting process will eventually damage them. I have found that having a good brush that is the right size for the task is the greatest help in putting the dye where I want it with the effect that I want. If I use a tiny brush to cover a large area, for example, the effect will be completely different from that achieved using a large brush. The following list suggests some tools you may want to try. Chapter 5 will give more details about applications.

Possible Tools

    Bristle brights, sizes 1, 4, 8
    Nylon rounds, sizes 000, 2, 4, 6
    Nylon brights, sizes 4, 8, 12
    Sponge brushes, 1", 2", 4"
    Fine-tipped syringes or squeeze bottles
    Sponges
    Plastic stencils
    Pipe cleaners
    Carved or plain wood blocks
    Clear, self-adhesive plastic
    Different widths of tape
    Spray bottles
    Silk screen equipment

WORK SPACE

The work space you need depends on how much fabric you want to dye paint at once. I like to have the whole piece of fabric fit on the table top, so when I work on a three-yard piece, I get out the pingpong table in the playroom. However, it is a fairly simple matter to work on a yard at a time, and that doesn't require a huge space. I recommend starting smaller and working on fat quarters (about 18" x 22"), to get the feel of how the dye goes on the fabric. Avoid tiny or very narrow pieces of fabric because they are awkward to wash.

When the fabric is wetted, with dye or water, it becomes transparent and stretches. For this reason, I work on a washable, white surface so the colors are easy to see. Many artists stretch fabric over a wooden frame before dyeing it. Suspending the fabric above the work surface is an unnecessary step, because when the dye is applied with the thickened print mix, it does not flow through the fabric the way that water does. When I use a very thin dye mixture and want it to move around, there is no advantage in stretching the fabric so it doesn't touch the work surface. Imagine a 45" square piece of fabric on stretcher bars: the wetter it gets, the more it sags down in the middle. The fabric bounces, and a firm, straight line is very difficult to paint. Instead, the fabric can be stretched directly on the white surface with tape. As the fabric gets wetter, the tape can be moved to pull out any wrinkles. If the shape of the image can be dis-

Right:
In my workroom, I am printing silk scarves from a design created on the tabletop, then stacking them in layers on plastic beneath the table.

Left:
Painting with the cotton unstretched. It is laid on a piece of plastic so it can be moved around on the table and allowed to hang over the edges without smearing.

Below:
Thickened dye being painted directly on cotton which is stretched on a white board.

torted by stretching, make sure that it is drawn on the fabric before the fabric is stretched. When the fabric is washed, it will resume its woven shape. In order to make use of a small space, I have various sizes of ⅛" masonite with one side enameled white. While I am waiting for one piece of fabric to be dry enough to take it off, I can move the board with the fabric taped to it, stand it against the wall, and work on another piece. If the dye is laid on thick and wet, the board may need to be laid flat to avoid dripping. This method also offers the option of going back to work on it later without having to stretch the fabric again. If the design is on a large piece of fabric and requires detailed work, it may be easier to work with it unstretched. That way, the part being painted can be close to you, and it can be moved around without your having to reach too far. Other times, you may want to wrinkle, pleat, or twist the fabric before painting. Then very large pieces can be dye painted without such a large work surface.

Chapter 4

THE COLORS

Color Theory And Dyes

Practical Applications Of Dye Chemistry

Color Mixing Exercises

COLOR THEORY AND DYES

Procion® MX dyes are ideal for mixing a great variety of colors that vary in hue, value, and intensity, because they have a high level of brightness, many colors, and good mixing ability. You do not need to know a lot of theory in order to have success at creating colors with Procion® MX dyes, because what you see on the fabric is very close to what the final color will be. After dye painting fabric for many quilts, however, I began to find it useful to understand how color theory relates to dyes in order to be able to predict even more exactly what colors I am mixing. The following is a brief explanation for dyers who want to know *why*.

The color wheel is a theoretical illustration of the colors we see based on pure color's reflection of light. The three points of the triangle are the most intense colors, primary colors. Pure red, for example, has no yellow or blue reflected with it. Primary colors, in theory, are ones that cannot be mixed using any combination of other colors, and ones that are used in making colors other than primaries. Inside the circle, the colors become less intense; that is, red with a small amount of blue reflected with it is not as intensely red. If the red also has a small amount of yellow in it, it will appear even less intense. In the real world of dyes, there is no such thing as a pure color; there is no dye that reflects only pure red, for example, so all of the red dyes are already slightly lower in intensity than the pure red of color theory. Procion® MX dyes have a high degree of brightness or intensity compared with other dyes. That is, they do reflect a fairly pure color. Natural dyes produce muted colors, or colors of low intensity, because the light reflected by these dyes is a mixture of colors, not a pure color. Bright colors cannot be produced starting with colors of low intensity. Synthetic dyes are frequently associated with bright, "unnatural" colors because they are often not mixed at all. Creating earth colors with subtle variations in value or intensity using Procion® MX dyes is entirely possible; it just takes practice using different proportions of dye colors and print mix.

The fullest intensity of any color is dyed using only one unique chemical dye, called a self color. Many self colors of Procion® MX dyes have been developed, so the dyer has quite a few choices of colors that are actually different chemicals, not just many mixtures of only a few chemicals. In practice, the result for the dyer is the possibility of mixing colors using more than one red dye. Mixing *fuchsia*, bright yellow, and blue will result in a wide range of colors. Mixing *red*, bright yellow, and blue will create a different range of colors. The same is true of yellow and blue. Mixing with *golden yellow* will result in a different range of colors than mixing with *bright yellow*. In the Procion® MX series, red,

*Opposite page:
Yellow, red, and blue painted across each other create secondary colors.*

yellow, and blue each have several self dyes, so the intensity or brightness of the colors created from them can be kept high. For that reason, self dyes, ones that are a pure chemical and not already a mixture, are best for creating a varied range of intense colors.

PRACTICAL APPLICATIONS OF DYE CHEMISTRY

There is a publication in five volumes called the *Colour Index*, produced by U.S. and British dyers, that catalogues all dyes according to use, class, structure, and commercial names, so that each can be identified with a generic name. Imperial Chemical Industries (ICI) is the only manufacturer of Procion® dyes; they still hold the patents. However, distributors often give their own brand names and color numbers to Procion® dyes. You don't need to look up the *Colour Index* codes, because you should be able to get the *manufacturer's number*, which corresponds to the color numbers the dye distributor uses. The manufacturer's number

Below:
These colors were mixed using only the same bright primary colors shown in the photo on the opposite page.

"Procion® Red MX-8B," for example, indicates the brand, color, reactive group, and a code that indicates the direction the color leans, in this case, very blue. "Procion® Red MX-5B" is not as blue. Using this number you can tell whether a dye is the identical type and color as others. The distributor should also be able to tell you whether a color is a self dye or a mix.

When mixing colors, it would seem logical to expect a "real orange" if you mix equal parts of red and yellow, and likewise, a "true green" and "true purple" if equal parts of the appropriate primaries are mixed. The actual case is illustrated in the color wheel of dye-painted cotton (shown on page 36). The primaries were measured and mixed in proportion to their placement in the triangle: the secondary color nearest each primary has three parts of that color and one part from the other corner; the middle colors along the lines have two parts of each primary. Red is very strong, and overpowers yellow, so an orange will be achieved by mixing *much less* red with yellow than even one part red to three parts yellow. Blue is very dark and impacts yellow very quickly, but red is so strong that a mixture of even one part red and three parts blue creates a purple that leans to the reddish. The theoretical middle of the color wheel is black, but as shown in the middle colors of the triangle, the only color like black is closest to the blue corner. The four small triangles in the middle were mixed with the same values as the outer squares; they would need to be mixed with a greater concentration of dye to get the dark value of a black.

Not all dyes have the mixing ability of the Procion® dyes. Even though each Procion® MX color is a different chemical with individual characteristics such as reactivity, affinity for the fiber, and solubility, these colors can all be mixed and used together. (As explained in Chapter 1, the Procion® MX series is very different from Procion® H, and they should *not* be mixed.) This fact allows the dyer to mix a huge variety of colors from the brightest to the most subtle. However, the dyer should be aware that because each color is a different chemical, some dyes have special characteristics that influence color results.

Procion® Turquoise MX-G is often used as a primary to create bright colors of green and violet. I used it to mix colors for several years, but as I became more focused on exact color matching, I realized that after I washed the fabric, the colors seemed to be different, less blue than they had appeared before washing. The reason for this is that the turquoise dye molecule is much larger than the others and needs more energy to react with the fibers. This means that in immersion dyeing, a hotter dyebath is required, and in dye painting, more time is needed. Turquoise mixed with a little yellow looks much more blue before it is washed than after because the yellow reacts proportionally more than the turquoise. When I want to be able to judge the color as I paint, I do not mix with turquoise; too much washes out for me to predict the final color. When I want that bright turquoise that cannot be mixed from any other combination, I use the turquoise self dye.

I found that I could mix a deep black with turquoise, fuchsia, and bright yellow; but after it was washed and some of the unreacted turquoise had washed out, the fabric was brown. Black is a very difficult color to achieve with dyes. If black is created by mixing the three primaries, a light value is often the result. The color may be correct, but if the value is too light, it will be gray instead of black. The dye mix needs to be made as concentrated as possible, and sometimes the area needs to be overpainted in order to achieve the depth of color required for black. All the black dye powders are some mixture of a red, a yellow, and a blue, and they produce different colors of black: greenish black, reddish black and so on. PRO Chemical and Dye, Inc. makes Pro Cotton Black 602, which will produce a deep black when dye painted on both cotton and silk. When I make the dye stock for black, I double the powder in the same amount of water and urea to make the stock more concentrated. As with turquoise, I do not mix with black because the final color is not predictable enough. Using a more concentrated dye stock, the color mixed appears much darker on the fabric before washing than after.

The color wheel is a good reference, but the best predictions of color will be based on fabric samples you have kept. Equal parts of red and yellow do not make an orange that is visually halfway between the two. Each dye's chemical make-up will influence the way it reacts; one yellow may work faster or at a lower temperature than another. A good way to record what colors do to each other is to think of them in proportions. How many parts yellow to how many red make your favorite orange? Record the manufacturers numbers for the red and yellow used. Mix them together in the palette or mix them on the fabric by overpainting. If you always use the same red, yellow, and blue for mixing colors, it is easier to recreate colors you have mixed before. The same is true of paints on paper: color mixing just takes practice.

Even when white fabric is used, a lot of variables influence the final colors after dyeing: the

Below:
These fans were dye painted on silk using bright yellow, turquoise, and fuchsia. The overlapping of these dyes created the other colors.

Right:
Circles are primary colors, squares are secondary colors, and triangles are mixtures of all three primary colors.

Opposite page, bottom:
Each primary is mixed with the other two primaries to create some of the possible secondary colors.

density and structure of weave, the exact fiber content (cotton, silk, linen, rayon), the color of the fabric, and any treatments it has been given such as bleaching and mercerization. Samples should be made on the actual fabric. The process that is used will also influence the color. For those who have done a lot of immersion dyeing, it is important to know that the proportions used to create a color by immersion dyeing will be somewhat different from those used in the dye painting process because the dye/water ratio influences the reaction rate of the dyes. Samples of the fabric before and after washing should be kept, because seeing the difference after the washing process will help the dyer anticipate the slight value change. Studio conditions during the curing process and any idiosyncrasies of the particular dyes used can also be evaluated by keeping samples.

COLOR MIXING EXERCISES

Try the following color mixing exercises to learn more about the ways you can work with dyes. Start with one of each primary color. For yellow, use bright Yellow MX-8G, medium Yellow MX-GR, or golden Yellow MX-3RA. For a red, use Fuchsia MX-8B or Red MX-5B. For a blue, use Blue MX-R, Turquoise MX-G, or Navy MX-4RD.

Refer to Chapter 2, steps 1, 2, 3, and 4, to prepare the fabric, print mix, and dye stock. Mix a small amount of the red stock (about 1 tablespoon) with an equal amount of print mix, in a small cup, and do the same with the yellow and blue dye stocks. Don't measure, just approximate the amounts. From here on, the precise measuring and mixing is over; just judge by eye and enjoy. The illustrations for this chapter use Yellow MX-8G, Red MX-8B, and PRO Blue 404, which is similar to Blue MX-R.

• MIX A VALUE GRADATION

EXERCISE: The purpose of this exercise is to find out how much dye it takes to make different values of the same color. Use red or blue, because yellow is so light that its values are harder to see. Paint a stroke of the dye mix prepared as on page 36, directly on the fabric. That is your darkest value. Put one brushful of the color on the palette and add an equal amount of clear print mix (one brushful). Stir well to blend, and paint a second stroke of that second value on the fabric next to the first. Take a brushful of this second value and put it in another place on the palette. Add about the same amount of clear print mix to it, stir and apply this third value on the fabric. Continue until the color is very pale.

Notes about value:

Transparent colors always look darker when they are wet than when they are dry. This is something your eye will adjust to with practice.

The only way to paint a darker color of this exact color is to overpaint it, when it is either wet or dry, or after it has been cured, washed and soda-soaked again. Try it.

Above:
Three primary colors
diluted with print mix
to create lighter
values of each color.

• MIX A COLOR GRADATION BETWEEN TWO PRIMARIES.

EXERCISE: Your purpose is to see the range of colors between the primaries. Start with red and paint a stroke of it on the fabric. Put one brushful of the red on your palette and add a *tiny* amount of blue. Mix well and paint it on the fabric next to the first red stroke. The second color will still be red unless a lot of blue was added. Continue adding *small* amounts of blue. The color will shift as gradually as the second color is added. Continue until the final color is blue. If streaks occur in the samples, the dye in the brush has not been sufficiently mixed.

EXERCISE: Do the same with yellow and blue, and yellow and red. It is easier to see the color shift if you start with the lighter color and add the darker.

Right:
Mixing complemen-
tary colors creates
colors of less inten-
sity: note the result of
red mixed with green,
and blue mixed with
orange.

• Mix A Complement Gradation, Using All Three Colors.

The purpose of these exercises is to see the grayed colors that occur as a color and its opposite across the color wheel are mixed.

Exercise: Paint a stroke of the red primary on the fabric to show your starting color. Mix a green in the palette and add a *tiny* amount of it to the red. Stir thoroughly and paint a stroke on the fabric next to the red. Continue adding *small* amounts of green to the red and on the fabric paint a stroke of each new color. Continue until the final color is green. The number of colors created and how gradual the steps are between them will depend on the amount of green added at each step. The second and third strokes of color should still be in the range of red. If you jumped to gray or brown, you added too much green.

Exercise: The complement of yellow is purple and the complement of blue is orange. Try them!

Exercise: Theoretically, black should occur in the middle somewhere. See how close you can get. Judge the color after it is dry and again after it is washed. If you can't achieve a hue of black that you like, try mixing with a self navy or another red or yellow.

Note about mixing complements:

The exact color of the complement will determine the range of colors produced. For example, adding a very yellowish green to red will create a very different range of colors than adding a very bluish green. Adding red-violet to yellow will create warmer hues than adding blue-violet.

Right:
Yellow mixed with
red-violet and blue-
violet creates different
color ranges.

• MIX THREE PRIMARIES ON THE FABRIC.

The purpose of these exercises is to see the results of mixing the colors directly on the fabric. For example, when blue is painted over yellow it creates a lighter green than when yellow is painted over blue.

EXERCISE: Start with the three primaries mixed in equal parts with print mix. Using a wide brush, paint a vertical line of clear print mix, then paint a vertical line of yellow, red, and blue on a piece of fabric. Then paint a horizontal line of the same three colors across them. The color will smear more or less, depending on how much dye is applied in the brush stroke and how much time is allowed for the dye to soak into the fabric. Clean and squeeze out water from the brush each time. To make it easier, use a different brush for each color.

EXERCISE: Do the same exercise using a light value of yellow, red, and blue for the horizontal lines.

Notes about overpainting the dyes:

The first dye on the fabric is likely to have the greatest impact on the final color of the fabric.

Even clear print mix dilutes later applications of color and acts as a light resist. Very thick print mix resists even more.

Painting over wet dyes has a different result than over dry. Knowing these results can help you create the effect you want.

Below:
When overlapped, primary colors create a third color. Clear print mix painted on the fabric makes a lighter value of the colors painted on afterwards.

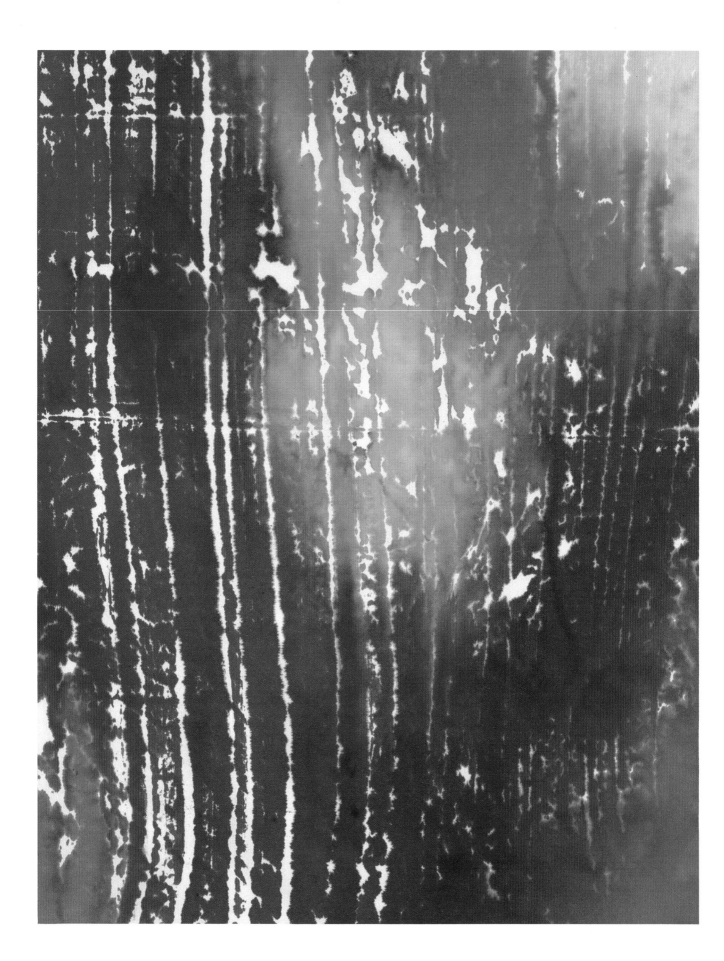

Chapter 5

THE APPLICATIONS

Using Brushes

Using Other Tools To Apply Dye

Using Print Techniques

Using Resist Techniques

Using Fabric Manipulation Techniques

Using Combinations Of Techniques

This chapter presents a series of exercises which introduce various tools and techniques that can be used to manipulate dyes. Actually doing the exercises will be more informative than just reading about them. At the same time, you can use your favorite colors and practice mixing them. Do several samples on one piece of fabric so the washout process will be easier. Consider the exercises a starting place for more ideas. *Keep Samples.*

USING BRUSHES

• PAINT A SOLID.

EXERCISE: Paint with the darkest value of any color, using a thick dye/print mixture and a flat, stiff brush. Work evenly, using a large brush for larger pieces. A sponge brush will create a smoother surface than a bristle brush; rub the color with a paper towel to smooth if needed. The color will be as even as you apply it. If you apply more dye to one place, it will be darker than where you apply it thinly.

Opposite page:
Monoprinting on cotton broadcloth using only the three primaries and blending them on the printing surface.

Left:
Paint evenly to create a smooth, solid color. This is harder to do with light values.

EXERCISE: Mix more print mix into a small amount of the dye you used in the previous exercise, to create a pale value of the same color. Now paint a solid. The lighter values require more care to make them even, because more color is added to places where the brush strokes overlap.

Above:
Painting a smooth,
continuous gradation
takes practice, espe-
cially on a large area.

Below:
Plaids involve over-
lapping colors and
different line sizes.

• PAINT A CONTINUOUS GRADATION.

EXERCISE: Paint a thin, even layer of clear print mix on stretched fabric. Before it dries, start painting color on top of it, working evenly in horizontal brush strokes. Start at the middle of the fabric with a medium value of the color and blend it down with gradually lighter strokes; then go back to the middle and add a darker value, blending it downward over the first color. If you get too much thickener on the fabric, your strokes will leave lines. The fabric can be blotted with a paper towel to take off some moisture (and dye) and worked over until you are satisfied. Start again at the middle with another color and do the same working upwards.

The texture you create is largely determined by how you manipulate the dye. A smooth gradation over a large surface takes practice and bigger brushes. If you find streaks that look much darker, you missed those areas with the original coating of print mix, and the dye penetrated directly to the fabric. The print mix provides a medium in which to manipulate the dye before it penetrates the fabric, and at the same time, it dilutes the value of the color. The same blending technique can be used on any area of fabric that has been painted, keeping in mind that the color underneath will influence the value and color of the one going on top.

• PAINT A PLAID.

EXERCISE: Mix four or five colors of different values with a medium-to-thick dye/print mixture. Combine vertical and horizontal lines of different widths, leaving white showing if you wish. Paint them diagonally for a plaid on the bias; then you will be able to cut squares that have a diagonal design without bias edges. Remember, the darker colors will smear if wet: paint towards them or wait until they are dry to the touch before crossing them with a brush.

EXERCISE: Use the same colors and create a completely different plaid by varying the line widths, the wetness, and the values.

• PAINT A PATTERN.

EXERCISE: With a soft, round brush and a sponge brush, paint a repeat pattern on a piece of white fabric or over one of the pieces you have already painted. Use a dye/print mixture that is medium to thin in consistency. You might use a 6B pencil to make light pencil lines as approximate guides. (I find that the 6B pencil disappears in the washing step.) Remember that the flow of the dye is determined by how thick the print mix is, whether you are working on wet or dry fabric, and how much dye you apply on the fabric.

EXERCISE: Try creating a repeat pattern using the shape of the brush itself as a stamp.

• PAINT A HARD-EDGE DESIGN.

EXERCISE: Use a pencil to draw simple shapes on your fabric, some straight lines, some curves, nothing too small. Use a flat bristle or nylon brush and a dye/print mixture that is medium to thick in consistency. Paint each area a solid color, practicing smooth strokes. Use a smaller brush or a pointed brush when needed, especially in corners. If you do not overlap the colors, they will not bleed together. If they do, your mixture is too thin or you have laid on too much dye in one spot. Letting one color dry before painting next to it is the easiest way to achieve a firm division between the two colors, although with practice, it can be done wet next to wet. Changing the size and type of brush as necessary will improve your accuracy.

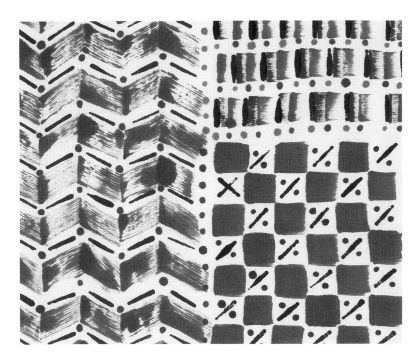

Above:
The options are limitless, once the brush becomes a pattern maker.

Below:
For hard-edge designs, take the time to paint the dye exactly where you want it to be.

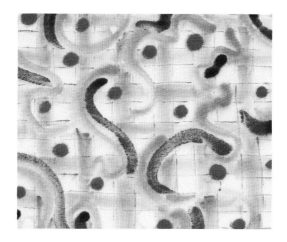

Right:
A medium/thin dye mixture painted on wet cotton, directly after immersion in the soda ash solution, creates blurry lines.

Right:
A sponge was dipped in a thick mixture of red and stamped on the dry cotton; then urea water and blue dye were gradually added to the red. As the mixture got thinner, the dye moved out of the stamped shape more, creating a halo effect.

Right:
Careful blending creates the illusion of shadows, giving depth to an object. Remember to keep some areas light because you cannot take away dye; to make an area appear lighter you can only make other areas darker.

• PAINT A SOFT-EDGE DESIGN.

EXERCISE: Work on the wet fabric, before the soda solution is dry. *Or* wet the fabric lightly with urea water and then apply the dye/print mixture either thick or thin. Too much urea water on the fabric will wash out the soda. The thinner the print mix, the more the colors will run.

EXERCISE: Mix the dye/print mixture very thin by adding urea water to the print mix; then add the dye stock and paint. The color will bleed out of the brush stroke; the thinner the print mix, the more it will run. You can dilute it down to almost the consistency of water. Remember to use urea water to thin the print mix before you mix in the colors. Adding just urea water after the color is mixed will make the color lighter in value. With some colors, after the dye is applied to the fabric in a very thin mixture, you will notice a halo of another color around the edges. This happens with the mixed colors, and it is an effect you may want to take advantage of. In order to avoid it, you need to work fast with large brushes, covering the area quickly, or use a thicker print mix.

EXERCISE: Paint the fabric evenly with clear print mix or any light color. Press a paper towel over the whole piece to lift off some of the moisture, and paint over it while it is still wet.

• PAINT A SHADED, THREE-DIMENSIONAL OBJECT.

EXERCISE: Draw a shape on the fabric with a pencil. If you have a photo or an actual object to look at, it will help you know where to put the shadows and highlights. Or just imagine an apple or a cube. Paint the image using a medium-to-thick dye/print mixture. I usually paint in the lightest areas first so I remember where they are. You can always make an area darker, but you cannot make it lighter! Before the surface dries, use dark colors to paint in the shadows, smoothing and grading them into the other colors. If the surface is very wet, it can be blotted with a paper towel. Cover it lightly with plastic if you wish to work on it later. When I paint a large area, if it seems to be drying too quickly, I cover the part I am not working on. If the fabric is too heavily saturated with dye and then covered, the dye may move and blend along the edges.

Left:
Straight lines and square corners are difficult to achieve on a miniature scale because of the nature of a brush line.

• PAINT DETAILS.

EXERCISE: Use a round nylon brush, #0 or smaller, and a dye/print mixture that is thin enough to paint a tiny dot or a very fine line. Draw a curving line with a pencil and then paint it as thin as possible. Add tiny leaves using just the tip of the brush. Have a paper towel ready to blot the color if it runs out of your pencil line. Painting fine detail requires working with the dye/print mixture quite thin, just on the edge of control. It takes a light touch and practice, but a leaf ⅛" can have a stem and veins. A high degree of detail cannot be achieved on coarse fabric, so the most detailed work I do is on a fine, smooth weave. Draw a geometric design 2" square, such as quilt block. Try filling in the colors. I find straight lines and square corners are harder than curved line designs when working in miniature.

Below:
Miniature Baltimore Album quilt being dye painted on stretched silk broadcloth.

EXERCISE: Using the same dye/print mixture, try signing your name in cursive handwriting. Sometimes I find it best to go over it very lightly once and then go back to darken it and add the flourishes.

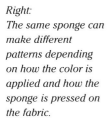

Right:
The same sponge can make different patterns depending on how the color is applied and how the sponge is pressed on the fabric.

Below:
A medium/thin dye mixture applied to a long piece of silk with household sprayers.

USING OTHER TOOLS TO APPLY DYE

• SPONGES

Use any kind of sponge, synthetic, natural, or cut into a shape. The sponge can be used as a stamp or a brush. For a firm clear mark, use the dye/print mixture fairly thick. The thinner the dye/stock mix, the more the dye will bleed away from the place you put it.

• SPRAYERS

Ordinary household sprayers can be used to apply a thin dye/print mixture to the fabric. Before spraying, the fabric can be folded, wrinkled, etc. to create a pattern. Overlapping different colors creates a soft blend, depending on how much you spray and how thin the mixture. If you let the first spraying get almost completely dry before the second, the colors bleed together less. Even though the mist is not very fine and the spraying is done quickly at arm's length, you should work with good ventilation – outdoors, out of the wind, for example. A dust or vapor mask should also be used.

• SYRINGES, SQUEEZE BOTTLES

Very thin lines can be made using a squeeze bottle or plastic syringe with a very tiny hole and a thick dye/print mixture. The line will spread a little, depending on how much dye was laid on the fabric. If the dye/print mixture is thinner, it will spread more. The quality of the line is determined by how quickly you move your hand; you will make dots when moving quickly, and blobs when you hesitate. The line also depends on whether you are painting over wet or dry fabric. Use a straight edge if you want to make a very straight line.

- STAMPS

Make your own stamps out of anything you can carve: erasers, cork, sponge, or wood. The only questions to work out are how well dye will adhere to the stamp and how to best apply dye to the stamp. The smoother the surface of the stamp, the less likely it is that the dye will stick. Try various ways: make a pad with layers of felt and soak it with the dye/print mixture, paint the dye on the stamp with a brush, roll the dye on the stamp with a soft brayer, or just dip the stamp into a flat dish of dye. Do whatever works best for the result you want.

Left:
Carve stamps for repeat designs: left to right, round wood block, self-adhesive rubber on a wood block, round sponge, wall paint applicator, square wood block.

- FOUND OBJECTS

Just about anything can be used as a brush or stamp. Find natural objects such as leaves, twigs, and pine cones, or household objects and odds and ends such as an empty spool of thread or a spatula. Putting something under the fabric will create a texture as you paint; try chicken wire, for example. String can be used as a brush, wetted with dye/print mix, and dropped on carefully or carelessly, dipped in multiple colors, etc. It can be laid under the fabric to create a texture or glued to a wooden block to create a stamp.

Left:
Look around you for different tools: left to right, dowel, spool, leaf, cedar branch, comb.

Left:
A syringe was used to apply red lines over the yellow and green dyes while they were still wet. Black lines were applied later, when the fabric was drier.

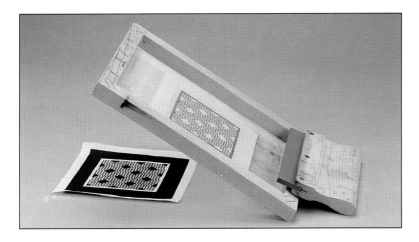

Above:
Fine patterns can be repeated using a silk screen and pressing the dye through the design onto the fabric.

USING PRINT TECHNIQUES

• SILK SCREEN

A thick dye/print mixture can be pushed with a squeegee through a design on a silk screen for a precise repeat image. For the most intense colors, such as black and navy, you might consider mixing the powdered dye directly into the print mixture instead of using the dye stock so the mix will stay very thick. Any type of silk screen technique can be used, from a simple design cut out of clear self-adhesive shelf paper to professional screens made from a photo-sensitive emulsion. Ordinary screen mesh (12XX) works fine for most purposes, but more attention to the size of the mesh and the thickness of the dye/print mixture is needed on very fine designs or on very fine fabric.

• BLOCK PRINTING

Deeply carved (or routed) designs on wood blocks work well with a thick dye/print mixture because the wood has texture to hold the dye and because the grooves are deep; a delicately carved linoleum block might not carry the design because the dye may fill in the grooves. Blocks can be made by gluing felt, rubber inner tubes from tires, cardboard, foam core, heavy cord, or self-adhesive stamping materials to wood blocks. A slightly padded work surface improves the contact between the block and the fabric, allowing the design to print more clearly. To keep the dye on the surface of the block design and avoid getting it in the grooves, use layers of felt saturated with the dye/print mixture as an ink pad or use a soft sponge brayer and a tray of dye/print mixture to roll the color on the block. Then press the block hard onto the block or hammer it. Depending on how exact you want to be, you might create a precise repeat pattern or use the block as a texture under or over other colors and designs.

• MONOPRINTING

EXERCISE: Paint a design on a piece of fabric, and while it is still wet, lay another piece of soda-soaked fabric (either wet or dry) over it. Press evenly (or unevenly) and the design will transfer if it is very wet. Less dye will transfer if it is drier.

EXERCISE: After you lift a very wet piece of fabric off the work surface, another piece can be laid down to pick up the design that is left on the white board.

EXERCISE: Paint a design on a washable surface, then lay the fabric on the dye. Press the fabric with another flat surface if necessary.

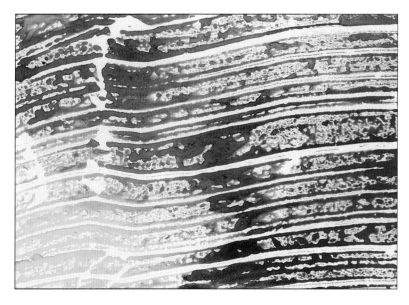

Above:
Viscose rayon printed from a design blended on the tabletop.

Left:
A China silk scarf printed from a design sprayed and poured on the tabletop.

Opposite page:
Make your own wood blocks for repeat patterns: the first two on the left are felt glued to wood, the next is string glued to wood, and the last is a routed piece of plywood.

Below:
Design created by
using cassava paste
as a resist then dye
painting over it. This
fabric was used in the
quilt entitled
INSIDE THE
HEXAGON, page 63.

USING RESIST TECHNIQUES

• WAX

Melting wax into the fabric to control where the dye penetrates is a traditional method called batik. Hot wax makes the most complete resist and creates the unique look of "crackle" where the dye enters the cracks in the wax. However, there are several disadvantages to using wax as a resist. Continuous use of hot wax requires a proper vapor-filtering mask, because when the wax is heated some of it floats in vapor form and can damage the lungs. Also, even a slight residue of wax on the fabric will affect later dyeing. Unremoved wax on the fabric over time gets a dull, powdery surface. It requires removal by ironing to melt out the major part of it and then boiling in soap (not detergent) or dry cleaning. If you wish, wax can be used effectively in combination with dye painting.

Cold wax is a resist to consider. It may not penetrate completely, but if a thick-to-medium dye/print mixture is used, the surface resist may be sufficient. Read the manufacturer's directions for removal and try a small amount first. Cold wax resists sometimes require a scrub brush, treatment with paint thinner or mineral spirits, or dry cleaning for complete removal.

• WATER-SOLUBLE RESISTS

Inkoyde Resist, cassava paste, and a variety of rice pastes used for traditional Japanese dyeing techniques are available. These are starch resists that will simply wash out while you are washing out the excess dye from the fabric. Each will have its own particular advantages. The Inkodye Resist is very thick and takes about a day to dry before you can paint over it. I have used it to create a completely clear resist in small areas, or a texture that is somewhat penetrated by the dye. It also works to some degree if it is thinned with water.

There are a variety of water-based resists available from dye and fabric paint distributors. Read and experiment first to see how much the resist penetrates the fabric, how hard it is to remove, and if it still resists when thinned.

• Gutta

Gutta is another type of resist used to hold the flow of liquid dyes within a design. It is most useful on thin fabrics like China silk; I do not know any type that penetrates cotton broadcloth. If the resist does not penetrate the fabric, the dye can flow around it. There are many different brands and types of Gutta. Many have a rubber base that is meant to leave a permanent line on the surface of the fabric. Some will gradually wash out and some will be removed by dry cleaning. Gutta can be combined with the dye painting process, but be sure to test it to see whether it will stick to the soda-soaked fabric or try applying it before the soda treatment. Experimentation with different brands is the only way to determine the results.

• Tapes and Cut-out Shapes

A resist can be created by laying a dye-resistant surface over the fabric or by sticking it to the fabric. Cutouts of clear, self-adhesive shelf paper, masking tape in different widths or cut in shapes, butcher paper with a waxed side, wax paper, or press-apply stickers can be used to paint, spray, or stamp over. A thin dye/print mixture will flow through the fabric and under the resist more than a thick mixture, so first determine what effect you want. The advantage of a transparent shape is that you can see how much dye has moved under it. Tape will create a hard line with a thick dye/print mix, especially if the tape is firmly pressed on and if care is taken to paint away from it, avoiding pushing the dye under the edge. If you want an absolutely straight line, however, with no irregularities, it is easier to paint it with a good, flat nylon brush than try to achieve it with a masking tape resist.

EXERCISE: Try cutting a stencil from a thin sheet of stiff plastic. Painting with a thick dye/print mix away from the cut edges and toward the inside of the design can create a fairly uniform design. Also try spraying on the dye through a simple stencil. If precision and many repeats are required, consider using the silk screen process.

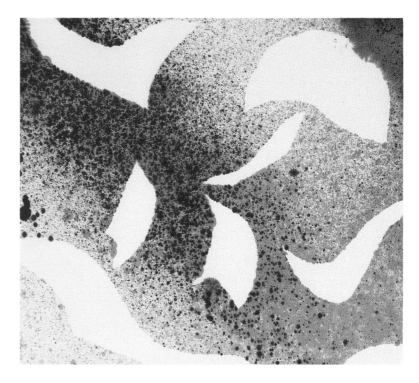

Above:
Clear self-adhesive paper was cut and applied to silk which was then lightly sprayed with a medium/thin dye mix.

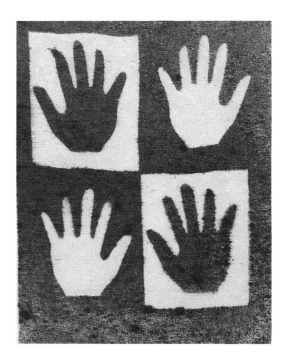

Left:
A plastic cut out was used as a stencil over silk noil, and the fabric was then sprayed.

Right:
A long piece of fabric pleated and taped to a board and the resulting fabric, after painting and washing.

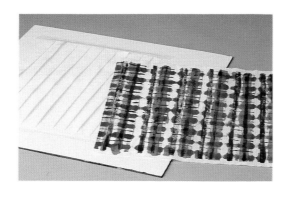

Right:
A long piece of fabric tied tightly with string, then painted with both thick and thin dyes and the results, after washing.

Below:
Silk was wrapped around a plastic tube and wound with plastic monofilament at about ½" intervals. Then the fabric was pushed together lengthwise to create folds, and dye painted. More of this piece of fabric is shown on page 7.

USING FABRIC MANIPULATION TECHNIQUES

• WRINKLES, FOLDS, PLEATS

Try manipulating the fabric before applying the dye. Smocking, pleating, gathering, folding, tying, and twisting all create different effects. The dye can be applied on manipulated fabric with brushes, syringes, spray bottles, or sponges. After the fabric is dyed, it can be rearranged and dyed again, either before or after it has cured.

• BOUND RESISTS

Tie-dyeing and bound resist methods traditionally used with immersion dyeing can be used with the dye painting method, using the same recipes I have described. When the dye is applied directly, the dyer has the advantage of applying different colors to different areas without always overdyeing them. Bind the fabric with string or plastic strips where you wish to reduce the penetration of the dye. Wrap fabric around objects such as tubes or marbles; tie and manipulate to create different patterns, then dye paint with a brush or sprayer. Different effects will result, depending on whether you are using a thin or a thick dye mixture.

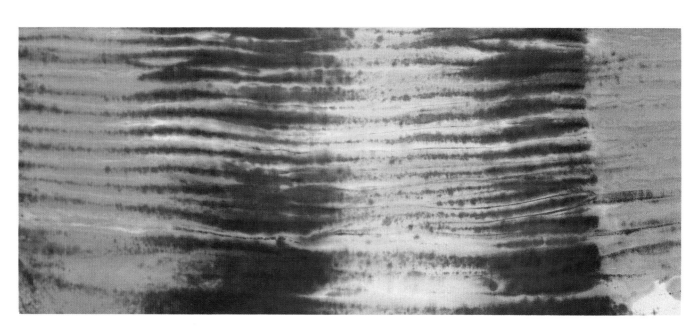

USING COMBINATIONS OF TECHNIQUES

• EXAMPLES

Dye painting techniques can be done in layers. If the first layer is dry, and a wet layer is applied over it, there is little or no movement of the first color, depending on the thickness of the print mix and the concentration of the color.

EXERCISE: Brush on lines of color and then use a syringe to apply finer lines over the brush strokes. There will be a difference between the type of line drawn by the syringe when it crosses wet fabric and that drawn when it crosses dry fabric. After curing, the dye/print mixture applied with the syringe will appear uniform in color, but after the fabric is washed, the line will be lighter where it crossed the other colors than where it crossed undyed fabric. The first application of dye/print mixture acts as a slight resist and the color blends visually with the second color, creating a third. The order of application of the dye can influence the results, particularly if a thick dye/print mixture is used. The more layers of color applied, the more difficult it is for the later colors to penetrate to the fibers and react, but the later colors will appear to have the greatest impact, until washout.

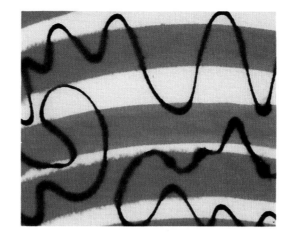

Left:
Black lines were applied over the wet red lines; where the black lines cross dry fabric they appear blacker and do not spread.

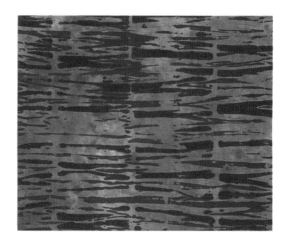

Left:
Silk dyed blue and purple, and then washed, gathered on the sewing machine, and dye painted using black and red.

Below:
The yellow line was applied first, in a thick mixture, to dry silk. When the fabric was almost dry, it was sprayed with yellow, turquoise, and fuchsia. The yellow line was barely visible until after washing.

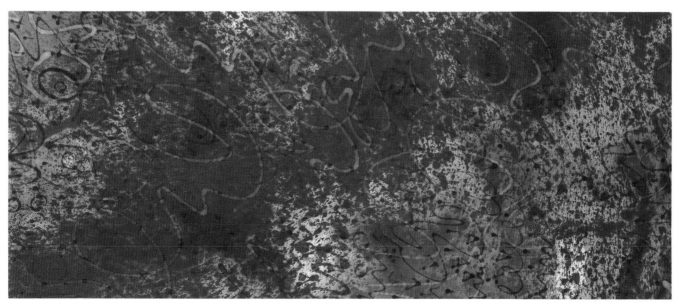

EXERCISE: Print a wood block design, let it dry, and apply the background color by painting or spraying, or do the reverse. If the first layer was dry, a later spraying will not necessarily make it bleed.

Another way to combine techniques is to apply the colors, and cure, wash and dry the fabric. Then soak it in soda again and apply more color. This way, color and value can be checked and adjusted fairly precisely in the second dyeing. The acid method, for silk only, (see page 23) avoids the soda treatments.

Above:
This silk noil was printed with wood blocks and allowed to cure and dry completely before being sprayed and allowed to cure again. Then it was washed.

Right:
Detail of
TRILLIUM TOO,
Ann Johnston, ©1990.
Hand quilting by
Diane Roberts.

The silk broadcloth was dye painted, cured, and washed several times in order to achieve the shading and values desired.

• LIMITS

The alkali required for the dye/fiber reaction is in the fabric in a specified concentration. If the dye is overlapped in very thick layers, or repeated layers of very runny colors are applied, the concentration of washing soda can be diluted so much that the area actually washes out much lighter than the surrounding colors. If the dye is to be applied by pouring or in globs, the washing soda in the fabric is washed away from some spots and the full dye reaction cannot occur. For using these generous methods, consider the variations for mixing the alkali directly into the dye/print mixture that are described in Appendix A. Because these methods are fairly fast, their short shelf life wouldn't be as crucial. Mixing the acid into the print mixture, as is done for dyeing only silk (see page 23), also avoids the problem.

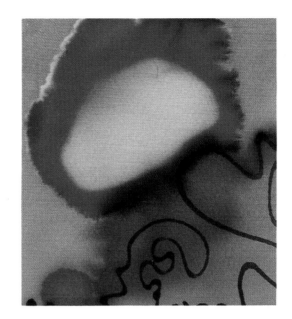

Left:
Before washing, this cotton was dark red and blue with no light areas. This photo taken after washing shows the areas where too much liquid was applied in one place.

Left:
Heavy cotton tablecloth fabric, monoprinted and painted with a brush.

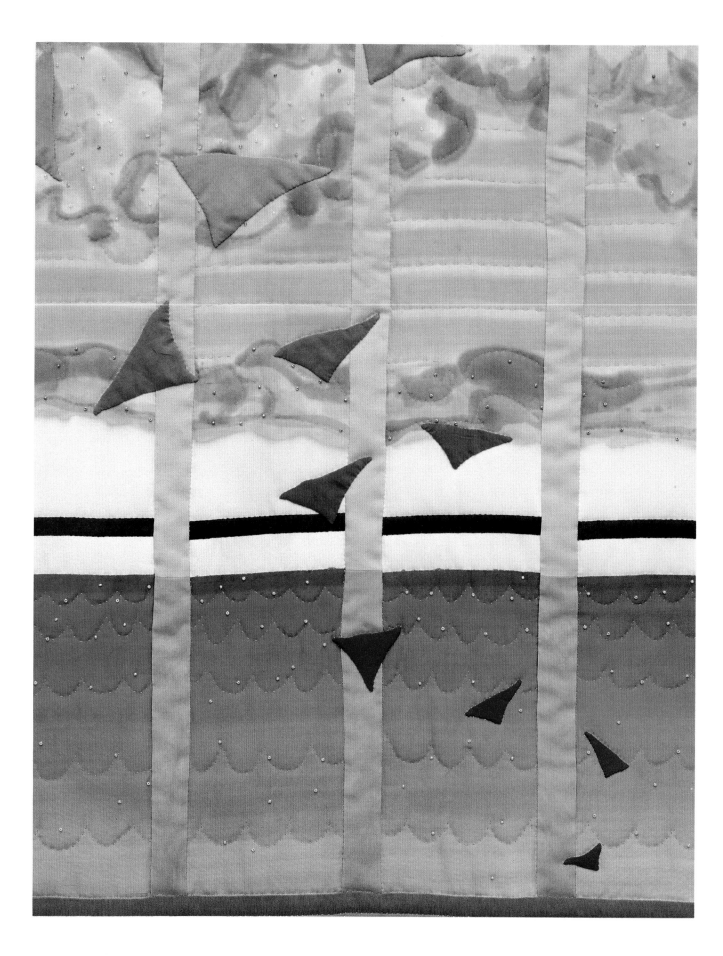

Chapter 6

GALLERY

Left:
ROOTABAGA SKY:
BIRDS IN FLIGHT V,
44" x 44",
Ann Johnston, ©1990.
Hand quilting by
Dorothy Campbell.

Dye painted and
immersion-dyed silk
broadcloth.

Opposite page:
Detail of
ROOTABAGA SKY:
BIRDS IN FLIGHT V,
Ann Johnston, ©1990.

The painted fabric
between the vertical
bars is not pieced; the
lines were painted
with a brush. The
triangles were
appliquéd afterwards.

Right:
ELEMENTS OF STILE,
31" x 32",
Ann Johnston, ©1991.

Dye painted and
immersion-dyed silk,
pieced, machine
quilted, dye painted
again, and washed.
Look at the stripes in
the blue sashing and
the grayed areas in
each block to see the
dye painting that was
done after quilting.

Left:
MERRY-GO-ROUND,
52" x 62",
Ann Johnston, ©1991.

*The horses were
painted on one piece
of silk over a period
of months, then
appliquéd over
the pieced and
appliquéd background
and borders. Hand
and machine quilted.
Embellished with fab-
ric paint, beads, and
rhinestones.*

Right:
MISSING PIECE,
29"x 29",
Ann Johnston, ©1991.
Hand quilted by Diane
Roberts.

Dye painted on silk
broadcloth, no piecing
or appliqué. The
missing puzzle piece
and more shadows
were dyed after quilt-
ing; then the quilt was
washed again.

Right:
CENTURY PLANT,
25" x 31",
Ann Johnston, ©1989.

Dye-painted silk;
hand quilted, bound
and framed.

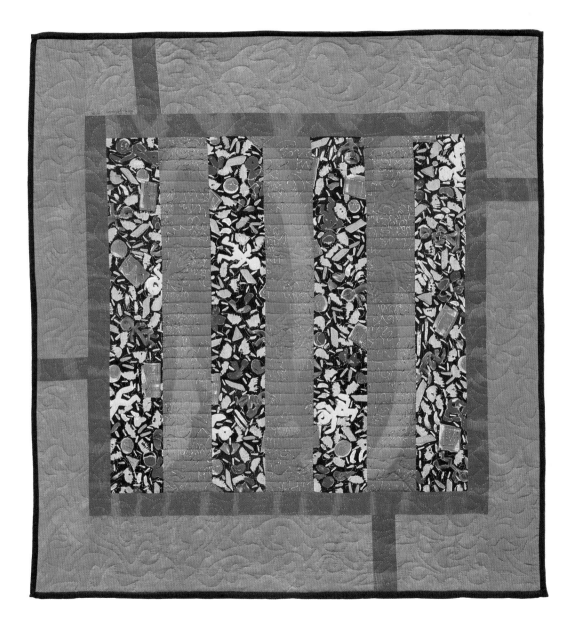

Left:
BARS VARIATION:
SELF-PORTRAIT,
48" x 52",
Ann Johnston, ©1990.

The center of the quilt
is dye-painted silk,
and the green border
was immersion-dyed
to match. Glitter paint
was squeezed on after
the center was pieced.
It is hand quilted with
silk and metallic
thread.

Right:
FOREST STAR,
30" x 38",
Ann Johnston, ©1990.
In the collection of the
Northwest Quilters.

Dye painted on silk.
Hand quilted with silk
thread.

Left:
INSIDE THE
HEXAGON,
42" x 61",
Ann Johnston, ©1990.
In the collection of
Sam and Kathryn
Imperati.

Dye-painted and
immersion-dyed silk
broadcloth; pieced,
hand and machine
quilted.

Right:
NIGHT DANCERS,
36" x 50",
Ann Johnston, ©1992.

Dye-painted cotton;
pieced. Sprayed and
painted with a
squeeze bottle; pieced
and machine quilted.

Left:
BAQ MINI, 1991,
8" x 8",
Ann Johnston, ©1991.
In the collection of
Michiko and Takashi
Nakato.

Dye-painted silk
broadcloth; hand
quilted with silk
thread.

Right:
This hooded wool
coat has dye-painted
silk facings which
inspired the embel-
lishments on the out-
side of the coat.

Right:
This silk noil skirt
and blouse were dye
painted with a syringe
and sponge brushes.
The placement of the
horizontal lines was
measured so the lines
would match along
side and back seams.

Left:
Cotton broadcloth coat. The sleeves were dye painted with notched brushes and spray bottles. The back and front were sprayed, washed, painted with a water-soluble resist, over-painted with black, and washed again. The rayon dress was immersion dyed to match.

Garment design and construction by Elaine Anne Spence.

Right:
Silk coat, pants, and blouse. The pieces of silk were monoprinted to fit the placement of the pattern pieces. The pants and blouse were immersion dyed to match.

Garment design and construction by Elaine Anne Spence.

Right:
Silk culottes and blouse. The fabric for the culottes was folded and sprayed with purple and green. Then it was washed and immersion dyed blue, with enough silk for the blouse. The triangles were made using sponges as stamps.

Garment construction by Elaine Anne Spence.

Left:
*Silk broadcloth jacket,
dye painted with
sponge brushes and
sprayer. Lining is silk,
folded and sprayed
golden yellow.*

*Garment design and
construction by Elaine
Anne Spence.*

Left:
*Detail of silk bomber
jacket. Using dye-
painted fabric, you
can change the
pattern or the color,
on the same piece of
fabric.*

Right:
Handmade books using dye-painted fabrics for the covers.

Book design by Ann Marra.

Right:
Cotton comforter and pillowcases. Each side of the comforter was painted as a whole piece, with the center seams finished. A narrow paint roller, sponges, syringes, and notched sponge brushes were used.

Far right:
100% white cotton napkins (hemmed) and matching table-cloth dye painted using brushes as stamps.

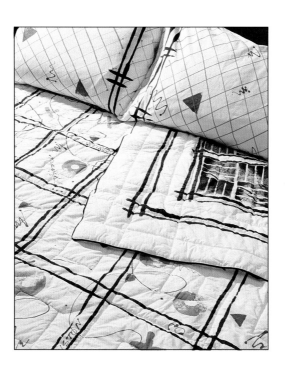

Left:
Cotton pillows:
monoprinting and
painting with brushes.

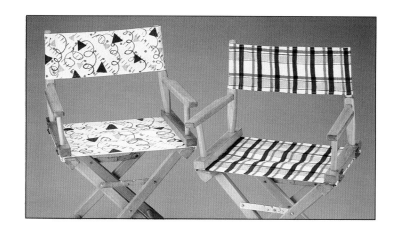

Left:
Using 100% cotton
canvas pieces,
director's chairs can
be soda soaked and
dye painted to match
anything. They will
fade with continued
exposure to sunlight,
just as the factory-
dyed ones do.

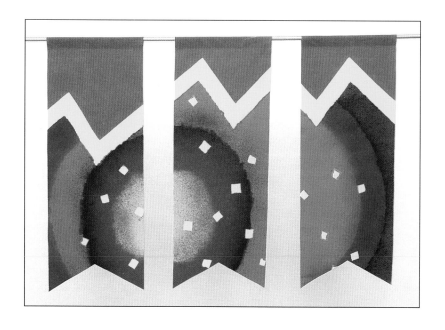

Left:
Heavy cotton banners,
20" x 48" each.
Sprayed and painted
with sponge brushes.

QUESTIONS & ANSWERS

1. What is the difference between dye and fabric paint?

Fabric paints, inks, and pens are often referred to as dyes because they color the fabric. However, they are actually pigments that are applied to the surface of the fabric, and they contain a binder to make the pigment adhere to the fibers. The binder is often a resin-like substance that requires heat treatment and usually adds a stiff layer to the fabric, particularly in large areas of intense color. Many paints have a binder that is designed to stick to fabric but not to itself, so experiment with any paint you want to use in layers.

Using fabric paint is the only way to add light areas to dark fabric and it can definitely be used on fabric after it has been dye painted (and washed). When you use fabric paints, you should consider the function of the fabric and how often it will be washed. There are many brands, all with different characteristics, and quality can only be judged by trial. In addition to considering the wash-fastness of the paint you should also consider the following: is it rub-fast, how does it feel to hand stitch through it, and how does it affect the overall texture and drape of the quilt or garment?

2. Why can't I just frame my dye painted fabric without washing it?

One important reason to use dye is to maintain the texture and weight of the fabric; the unfixed dye and chemicals fill and cover the weave of the fabric until it is washed. Also, the sodium alginate in the print mix is pure protein, and in combination with urea, which attracts moisture, the fabric will look dull and possibly even get moldy if not washed out. Even if no thickener is used, the excess dye that has not reacted with the fiber molecules will have poor lightfastness.

3. Why are colors lighter than I expected?

Add less print mix to the dye stock. Remember that transparent colors look much darker when wet than when dry. Hold the fabric up to the light and look through it when it is wet. What you see will be closer to what the value of the color will be when it is dry. Also, the dry color on the fabric will be slightly darker than it will be after it is washed. Some excess dye washes out, especially with the darker colors, but the dry value should be *very close* to the value after it is washed. If it is not, check for the following possibilities.

· Did you soak the fabric with the right amount of alkali?

· Could your fabric be a blend with a synthetic? Fiber-reactive dyes are not made for synthetics.

· What was the temperature of the area where you worked and where the fabric cured?

· How long did the fabric cure? Did it get completely dry, too soon?

· What is the density of the fiber in the fabric? If it is a lightweight batiste or China silk, the colors will not appear as dark as on fabrics that have more density.

· Did you use dye stock in which the dye

Opposite page: Silk broadcloth sprayed with gold, red, and turquoise dye. If you spray from one direction only, small wrinkles in the fabric create a secondary texture.

molecules had reacted with the water? Be sure it is fresh or constantly refrigerated.

4. Why did the white areas of my design turn slightly green (pink, blue, etc.) after washing?

This happens when you move to hot water too suddenly in the washout process, before the alkali has been completely removed. The excess dye circulating in the wash water can chemically bond with the fibers if any alkali is present, acting as a direct dye. These stained colors have only poor to fair wash-fastness. If the staining is not too bad, several hot washes with Synthrapol® SP could help.

5. Why is the dye bleeding out beyond my pencil line as I paint?

Control of the flow of the dye takes practice. The following are things to be aware of:
· After you wash the brush, squeeze out excess water with a towel.
· The line will spread more if the fabric is wet.
· Working with too much dye stock in the print mix makes the mixture too thin. *OR* if the print mix is diluted with too much urea water, the dye will flow away from the brush faster. Use a thicker dye/print mixture.
· You may simply be laying on too much dye in one spot. It requires a light touch with a brush to make a thin line.
· If you are working with a fairly thin dye/print mixture, be ready to blot the dye with a paper towel to control its flow.

6. How many layers of dye can I paint on top of each other?

The answer to this depends on the thickness of the dye/print mixture and what colors you use. The print mixture itself slightly resists the penetration of the dye to the fiber. One thick layer will resist and dilute the next layer of color considerably. If the first layer is navy blue,

a subsequent layer of yellow will not have much impact. If you layer the colors, practice will help you estimate the final color of the fabric. If layers of light colors are applied first and then black over all, the fabric will look black before it is washed, but not after! You may need to wash the fabric at some point, soak it in alkali again and then paint more.

7. Can I iron the fabric after it's been painted but not washed?

Allow time for it to cure and dry first. If the fabric has dried with wrinkles and lumps because it was not stretched and you want to work on flat fabric, iron it lightly. If you don't wait for it to cure first, the dyes won't have their fullest color. Sometimes it is harder to wash out the print mix after it has been ironed.

8. What ecological considerations are there in using and disposing of the Procion® MX dyes and related chemicals?

In the dye painting process, a very small amount of dye is used and about 90% of it is attached to the fibers when the correct curing is done. Any dye that does not react with the fiber is inert (no longer reactive) because it has bonded with water before dyeing or during the wash-out process. The other chemicals are similar to laundry products and can be handled accordingly. The alkali used in the dye process is not as strong an alkali as the cold water detergents we use. It is a mined product, a natural product of the earth. Sodium alginate is a protein extracted from seaweed and is harmless.

9. Can I use washing soda from the grocery store in the place of soda ash?

No. Washing soda sold as a laundry product is of undetermined strength and has additives such as bleach and perfume. It could influence the results you get with the dye process. Sodium carbonate is the chemical required, and the purer the form used, the more predictable the results. The same is true of water softeners if used in place of metaphos.

10. Should I warm the dye stock to room temperature before I paint?

I find that putting the amount of dye I will use during the day in the palette and putting the rest back in the refrigerator works well. By the time I have mixed my colors and started painting, it has warmed to room temperature. In any case, the layer painted on the fabric warms to room temperature fairly quickly. The temperature during the cure time is the essential element. Do not try to heat the dyes; temperatures over 100° will damage them.

Left:
I sprayed gold dye on a piece of gently puckered silk, and sprayed it again with orange and again with rust, rearranging it each time.

A New Starting Place

The advantage of dye painting is the immediacy of direct application of the dye to the fabric. This gives the artist freedom of expression in color, texture and design. The process can be used for large quantities and production printing methods, but more significant is the opportunity it offers the artist to create something unique, to make individual expressions rather than multiples. The method is flexible and open-ended. The fabrics that can be produced using exactly the same chemicals and supplies are tremendously varied, so the artist can concentrate on the content of the work rather than worry about all the different supplies that would be required using many different dyes and recipes.

What I can do with the dyes is expanding with experience and practice. The processes of mixing and painting have taught me to really see colors and know them. I would like to encourage other artists to experiment with painting with fiber-reactive dyes. Adjust the method to your needs and consider it one of many options in creating fiber art. Consider it also a process that will inspire ideas. An "accident" of dyeing may turn out to be the beginning of a new piece. After you experiment awhile, you will become comfortable with the method and it will become just one of the tools from which you can choose to solve a design idea or create a special fabric for a specific project. Other surface design techniques such as piecing, appliqué, beading, quilting, fabric paints, and embroidery can be combined with dye-painted fabric to create a unique expression of yourself, whether it is for quilts, garments, or other fabric art. You now have a new starting place.

Opposite page:
Silk noil, dye painted
with 1" sponge
brushes.

Appendix A

Variations Of The Process

USING OTHER RECIPES AND METHODS WITH PROCION® MX DYES

Fit the method to your needs! Each method of applying the Procion® MX dyes has advantages and disadvantages depending on your situation. The painting applications are the same and the results will be similar to the method I have described. The safety precautions and wash-out instructions are the same. See what works best for you.

• Using powdered dyes instead of dye stock.

Measure the dry powder directly into the print mix to the desired color and apply as desired to the presoaked fabric. Follow the same cure directions. *Use a dust mask.*

• Add alkali to the print mix (no pre-treatment of the fabric).

a. Make a dry mix of four parts sodium bicarbonate (baking soda) and one part sodium carbonate (soda ash). Mix thoroughly, store airtight.

b. Add dye stock (or powdered dye) to print mix to desired colors.

c. For each cup of dye stock and print mix, add 1 teaspoon of the above alkali mixture. You will add ⅛ teaspoon alkali if you are mixing only 2 tablespoons of a color. After the proper proportion of alkali is added, the colors can be intermixed. Add alkali to the clear print mix and urea water in the same proportions if you wish to change the value or density of your dye mixture.

d. The dye/alkali mixture will be full strength for only about *four hours*. If you use the mix after four hours, the fabric will appear to be the same colors, but more will disappear in the washing process.

e. Cover to retain at least some moisture, and cure 24 hours at room temperature.

• Use steam, no pretreatment of fabric and slow cure.

a. Mix dye with print mix to desired colors.

b. Add 1 teaspoon of sodium bicarbonate (baking soda) to each cup of the dye mixture.

c. Allow to dry completely. Steam iron all portions of the fabric two to three minutes or cure dried fabric in clothes dryer at hottest temperature for 45-60 minutes.

d. The dye/print mix can be stored refrigerated about three days, depending on the storage conditions.

USING OTHER FIBER-REACTIVE DYES

The other fiber-reactive dyes mentioned in Chapter 1 can be applied to the fabric directly and with the same painting techniques I have described already. You may find that one of them works better for your needs. A brief summary of the differences might help you decide.

*Opposite page:
Cotton broadcloth
dye painted with a
narrow sponge roller
starting with the
lightest colors first.
Hanging the fabric
while wet encouraged
the thickened dyes to
blend together.*

CIBACRON® F:

This dye is about half as reactive as the Procion® MX dyes, so it reacts more slowly with the water and can be stored longer. The practical shelf life of a dye in solution with water depends tremendously on the storage temperature. The recipes and applications are identical to those for Procion® MX dye; however, the curing time should be twice as long, 24-48 hours. Not as many self shades are available. Their higher prices reflect an import tariff.

LIQUID REACTIVE DYES:

These dyes are even less reactive than Cibacron® F dyes and require stronger alkali, higher temperatures, or longer curing time to achieve the fullest colors. The same methods of pre-treating the fabric with alkali or adding the alkali to the print mix can be used. The same painting techniques can be applied. For the air cure, the fabric needs two to three days in a warm, humid place (around 100°F). A steam iron, clothes dryer, or steamer can be used. If you use a steamer, the fabric has to be layered and wrapped carefully in clean newsprint to prevent condensation and transfer of the dyes. For me, the air cure at 100° was impossible, the ironing and dryer didn't set enough color, and the steaming of large pieces was too cumbersome. Another way to set the color involves painting on a very strong liquid alkali after the fabric is dyed. Then the fabric has to be sealed in plastic and cured 16 to 24 hours. I haven't tried it because some caution is required to handle such a strong alkali, and the cure process seemed likely to smear the colors and be especially cumbersome for large pieces of fabric.

Liquid Reactive dyes do not have as many self shades in red, but they do contain a self shade of black.

PROCION® H:

These dyes are the least reactive of the fiber-reactive dyes, so they can be stored longer in solution. The same principles apply as for the Liquid Reactive dyes. Like the Liquid Reactive dyes, Liquid® H dyes are not as economical as Procion® MX dyes because they are in a solution that is 60-75% water. They do not air cure without the liquid alkali treatment and are more demanding as to temperature and moisture content during the steaming process. I found the steam ironing option completely unsatisfactory, with too much color washing out.

"NEW" FIBER-REACTIVE DYES:

Check with the distributor; the "new" dye is one of the four types of fiber-reactive dyes, with a new name! Look at the reactivity rate and follow the distributor's directions. Compare the prices.

Appendix B

MAIL-ORDER SOURCES

Cerulean Blue, Ltd.
P. O. Box 21168
Seattle, WA 98111-3168
(800) 676-8602
(206) 323-8600

Dharma Trading Co.
P. O. Box 150916
San Rafael, CA 94915
(800) 542-5227
(415) 456-7657

Earth Guild
33 Haywood Street
Asheville, NC 28801
(800) 327-8448
(704) 255-7818

Exotic Silks
1959 Leghorn
Mountain View, CA 94043
(800) 345-7455, CA
(800) 845-7455, U.S.

Fab Dec
3553 Old Post Road
San Angelo, TX 76901
(915) 653-6170
(915) 942-0571

Nasco Arts and Crafts
901 Janesville Ave.
Fort Atkinson, WI 53538-0901
(800) 558-9595

PRO Chemical and Dye, Inc.
P. O. Box 14
Somerset, MA 02726
(800) 228-9393
(508) 676-3838

Rupert, Gibbon and Spider
P. O. Box 425
Healdsburg, CA 95448
(800) 442-0455
(707) 433-9577

Sax Arts and Crafts
P. O. Box 51701
New Berlin, WI 53151
(800) 558-6696, U.S.,
(800) 242-4911, WI

Sureway Trading Enterprises
826 Pine Avenue, #5&6
Niagara Falls, NY 14301
(416) 596-1887

Testfabrics
P. O. Box 420
Middlesex, NJ 08846
(908) 469-6446

Textile Resources
123½ Main St.
Seal Beach, CA 90740
(310) 598-6652

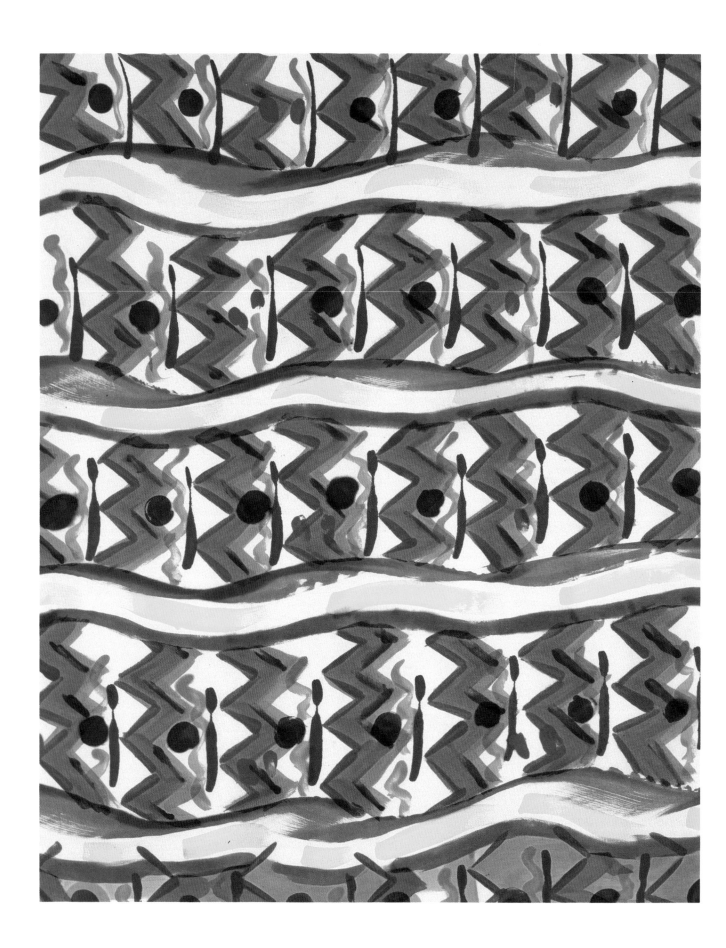

GLOSSARY

ACETIC ACID, 56% – concentrated liquid acid 11 times the strength of common vinegar; used with Procion® MX dyes for silk and wool.

BAKING SODA – sodium bicarbonate. Sometimes used in fixing dye-painted fiber-reactive dyes; weaker alkali than soda ash.

BINDER – chemical used to adhere color pigments to the surface of the fabric in fabric paints.

CELLULOSE FIBER – any fiber produced by a plant; having a chemical structure that can react with the fiber-reactive dye molecules.

CITRIC ACID – can be used in its crystal form to replace acetic acid for dye painting on silk.

COMPLEMENTARY COLORS – the colors directly opposite each other on the color wheel (red/green, yellow/purple, blue/orange).

DIRECT DYE – a dye for cellulose fabrics with weak chemical bonds between dye and fiber, having only poor to fair wash-fastness.

DYE ASSISTANTS – chemicals used to create conditions for the dye reaction; for example, soda ash for Procion® MX dyes on cotton; also called dye-activator.

DYE STOCK – a solution of dye in water. Adding urea to the dye stock allows a stronger concentration to be mixed.

FIBER-REACTIVE DYES – synthetic dyes that react with the fiber to create a strong chemical bond. They are used with cellulose fibers, silk, and wool. They require alkali or acid as a dyeing assistant in dye painting applications.

FIXATION – the stage of the dye process when the dye bonds with the fiber molecules.

GRADATION – gradual movement from one color to another.

GREIGE – fabric in an untreated condition, as it comes from the loom.

HAND – weight, texture, and drape of a fabric.

HUE – a specific color such as red, orange, or blue-green.

IMMERSION DYEING – the application of dyes with a large ratio of water to dye, for example, when Procion® MX dyes are used in a dyebath of salt and soda ash.

INTENSITY – the degree of brightness or dullness of a color; the purity of a color.

LUDIGOL® – trade name for the chemical used in dye painting applications of fiber-reactive dyes, to increase dye fixation during curing of fabric. It is a mild oxidizing agent. Also called sodium salt of m-nitrobenzene sulfonic acid, resist salts L or PRO Chem Flakes.

Opposite page:
Silk broadcloth
dye painted with
various brushes.

MERCERIZE – treat with caustic soda, giving the fiber greater strength, luster, and affinity to dyes.

METAPHOS – a chemical used in print mix when sodium alginate is used as a thickener, to make it flow better. It is also a water softener: sodium hexametaphosphate.

MIGRATE – spreading of dye to areas not intended.

PIGMENT – insoluble color-producing components of paints and inks, requiring a binder.

PRIMARY COLORS – the three basic colors from which all others are theoretically derived. For the dyer they are red, blue, and yellow.

PRINT MIX – the mixture of chemicals and water used in direct applications of fiber-reactive dyes. It can be mixed thin, like water, or thick, like paste.

PROCION® – trade name for fiber-reactive dyes manufactured by Imperial Chemical Industries and ICI America, Inc.

RESIST – anything used to prevent the penetration of the dye into the fiber, for example, wax, tape, rice paste.

SCOUR – cleaning fabric to remove any finish that might interfere with dye penetration.

SECONDARY COLOR – color produced when two primary colors are combined in any amounts (red + yellow = orange, red + blue = purple, blue + yellow = green).

SELF COLOR – dye color that is a single chemical, not a mixture of chemical dyes.

SHADE – a color plus black or one darkened by adding its complement.

SIZING – starch or other stiffener which is used on fabric to improve its appearance. It resists dye penetration.

SODA ASH – the alkali used for fixing fiber-reactive dyes, often referred to as washing soda. Also, sodium carbonate. PRO Dye Activator is a proprietary alkali mix that replaces soda ash and works in all geographic areas.

SODIUM ALGINATE F – the thickener used in print mix for use on silk, when very detailed lines are required.

SODIUM ALGINATE SH – the thickener used in print mix for both cotton and silk. Less needs to be used than with sodium alginate F.

SURFACTANTS – surface active agents in many detergents; they keep chemicals in suspension.

SYNTHRAPOL® *SP* – a concentrated surface active agent used with fiber-reactive dyes to prewash fabric and to wash out unreacted dye. It acts as a surfactant, keeping the unreacted dye in suspension and lessening the chance of staining.

TERTIARY COLOR – a color made up of any proportion of all three primaries, a color with less brightness because it has been dulled with the addition of the other two primaries.

TINT – a lighter value of a color; in dye painting, created by adding more print mix to the dye stock.

TRANSPARENT – capable of being seen through. With dyes, one color over another will result in a color that is a combination of both.

UREA – chemically formulated granules used in the dye painting applications of fiber-reactive dyes to keep the fiber moist, which is required for the dye reaction to occur.

VALUE – the degree of lightness or darkness of a color.

VISCOSE RAYON – rayon made from wood fibers; a cellulose fiber that can bond with fiber-reactive dyes.

Left:
Black lines
dye painted with a
notched sponge brush,
allowed to cure and
dry, and then sprayed
red and turquoise.

BIBLIOGRAPHY

Knutson, Linda. *Synthetic Dyes for Natural Fibers*, Madrona Publishers, Seattle, WA, 1982.

Meilach, Dona Z. *Contemporary Batik and Tie-Dye*, Crown Publishers, Inc., NY, 1973.

Proctor, Richard and Lew, Jennifer. *Surface Design for Fabric*, University of Washington Press, Seattle, WA, 1984.

Wiener, Don. "Procion® Cold Water Dyes," Pro Chemical and Dye, Inc., Somerset, MA, 1986.

Opposite page:
Silk, dye painted
with notched sponge
brushes, overlapping
colors.

∾ American Quilter's Society ∾
dedicated to publishing books for today's quilters

The following AQS publications are currently available:

- **Adapting Architectural Details for Quilts,** Carol Wagner, #2282: AQS, 1991, 88 pages, softbound, $12.95
- **American Beauties: Rose & Tulip Quilts,** Gwen Marston & Joe Cunningham, #1907: AQS, 1988, 96 pages, softbound, $14.95
- **America's Pictorial Quilts,** Caron L. Mosey, #1662: AQS, 1985, 112 pages, hardbound, $19.95
- **Applique Designs: My Mother Taught Me to Sew,** Faye Anderson, #2121: AQS, 1990, 80 pages, softbound, $12.95
- **Arkansas Quilts: Arkansas Warmth,** Arkansas Quilter's Guild, Inc., #1908: AQS, 1987, 144 pages, hardbound, $24.95
- **The Art of Hand Applique,** Laura Lee Fritz, #2122: AQS, 1990, 80 pages, softbound, $14.95
- **...Ask Helen More About Quilting Designs,** Helen Squire, #2099: AQS, 1990, 54 pages, 17 x 11, spiral-bound, $14.95
- **Award-Winning Quilts & Their Makers: Vol. I, The Best of AQS Shows – 1985-1987,** #2207: AQS, 1991, 232 pages, softbound, $24.9
- **Award-Winning Quilts & Their Makers: Vol. II, The Best of AQS Shows – 1988-1989,** #2354: AQS, 1992, 176 pages, softbound, $24.
- **Classic Basket Quilts,** Elizabeth Porter & Marianne Fons, #2208: AQS, 1991, 128 pages, softbound, $16.95
- **A Collection of Favorite Quilts,** Judy Florence, #2119: AQS, 1990, 136 pages, softbound, $18.95
- **Creative Machine Art,** Sharee Dawn Roberts, #2355: AQS, 1992, 139 pages, softbound, $24.95
- **Dear Helen, Can You Tell Me?...all about quilting designs,** Helen Squire, #1820: AQS, 1987, 56 pages, 17 x 11, spiral-bound, $12.95
- **Dyeing & Overdyeing of Cotton Fabrics,** Judy Mercer Tescher, #2030: AQS, 1990, 54 pages, softbound, $9.95
- **Flavor Quilts for Kids to Make: Complete Instructions for Teaching Children to Dye, Decorate & Sew Quilts,** Jennifer Amor #2356: AQS, 1991, 120 pages, softbound, $12.95
- **From Basics to Binding: A Complete Guide to Making Quilts,** Karen Kay Buckley, #2381: AQS, 1992, 160 pages, softbound, $16.95
- **Fun & Fancy Machine Quiltmaking,** Lois Smith, #1982: AQS, 1989, 144 pages, softbound, $19.95
- **Gallery of American Quilts: 1849-1988,** #1938: AQS, 1988, 128 pages, softbound, $19.95
- **Gallery of American Quilts 1860-1989: Book II,** #2129: AQS, 1990, 128 pages, softbound, $19.95
- **The Grand Finale: A Quilter's Guide to Finishing Projects,** Linda Denner, #1924: AQS, 1988, 96 pages, softbound, $14.95
- **Heirloom Miniatures,** Tina M. Gravatt, #2097: AQS, 1990, 64 pages, softbound, $9.95
- **Home Study Course in Quiltmaking,** Jeannie M. Spears, #2031: AQS, 1990, 240 pages, softbound, $19.95
- **Infinite Stars,** Gayle Bong, #2283: AQS, 1992, 72 pages, softbound, $12.95
- **The Ins and Outs: Perfecting the Quilting Stitch,** Patricia J. Morris, #2120: AQS, 1990, 96 pages, softbound, $9.95
- **Irish Chain Quilts: A Workbook of Irish Chains & Related Patterns,** Joyce B. Peaden, #1906: AQS, 1988, 96 pages, softbound, $14.95
- **The Log Cabin Returns to Kentucky: Quilts from the Pilgrim/Roy Collection,** Gerald Roy and Paul Pilgrim, #3329: AQS, 1992, 36 pages, softbound, $12.95
- **Marbling Fabrics for Quilts: A Guide for Learning & Teaching,** Kathy Fawcett & Carol Shoaf, #2206: AQS, 1991, 72 pages, softbound, $12.95
- **Missouri Heritage Quilts,** Bettina Havig, #1718: AQS, 1986, 104 pages, softbound, $14.95
- **Nancy Crow: Quilts and Influences,** Nancy Crow, #1981: AQS, 1990, 256 pages, hardcover, $29.95
- **Nancy Crow: Work in Transition,** Nancy Crow, #3331: AQS, 1992, 32 pages, softbound, $12.95
- **No Dragons on My Quilt,** Jean Ray Laury with Ritva Laury & Lizabeth Laury, #2153: AQS, 1990, 52 pages, hardcover, $12.95
- **Oklahoma Heritage Quilts,** Oklahoma Quilt Heritage Project #2032: AQS, 1990, 144 pages, softbound, $19.95
- **Quilt Groups Today: Who They Are, Where They Meet, What They Do, and How to Contact Them: A Complete Guide for 1992-1993,** #3308: AQS, 1992, 336 pages, softbound $14.95
- **Quiltmaker's Guide: Basics & Beyond,** Carol Doak, #2284: AQS, 1992, 208 pages, softbound, $19.95
- **Quilts: The Permanent Collection – MAQS,** #2257: AQS, 1991, 100 pages, 10 x 6½, softbound, $9.95
- **Scarlet Ribbons: American Indian Technique for Today's Quilters,** Helen Kelley, #1819: AQS, 1987, 104 pages, softbound, $15.95
- **Sensational Scrap Quilts,** Darra Duffy Williamson, #2357: AQS, 1992, 152 pages, softbound, $24.95
- **Sets & Borders,** Gwen Marston & Joe Cunningham, #1821: AQS, 1987, 104 pages, softbound, $14.95
- **Somewhere in Between: Quilts and Quilters of Illinois,** Rita Barrow Barber, #1790: AQS, 1986, 78 pages, softbound, $14.95
- **Stenciled Quilts for Christmas,** Marie Monteith Sturmer, #2098: AQS, 1990, 104 pages, softbound, $14.95
- **Texas Quilts – Texas Treasures,** Texas Heritage Quilt Society, #1760: AQS, 1986, 160 pages, hardbound, $24.95
- **A Treasury of Quilting Designs,** Linda Goodmon Emery, #2029: AQS, 1990, 80 pages, 14 x 11, spiral-bound, $14.95
- **Wonderful Wearables: A Celebration of Creative Clothing,** Virginia Avery, #2286: AQS, 1991, 184 pages, softbound, $24.95

These books can be found in local bookstores and quilt shops. If you are unable to locate a title in your area, you can order by mail from AQS, P.O. Box 3290, Paducah, KY 42002-3290. Please add $1 for the first book and 40¢ for each additional one to cover postage and handling.